101 Meditations for Life, Business and Bedroom Success

Rebecca Lowrie

Disclaimer

The author, Rebecca Lowrie, is American by birth and British by choice.

When deciding whether to write in an American or British voice, she chose to go with how she would speak. Well, actually, she did what any self-respecting author would do — she asked the hive mind of Facebook what they would do.

After a rigorous conversation* with people of different nationalities and opinions, Rebecca decided the most authentic thing to do was to be herself. That means there is a mix of American and British words, spellings and phrases in the book.

*Okay, a lot of teasing and British people saying 'arse'.

"If you must look back, do so forgivingly.
If you must look forward, do so prayerfully.
However, the wisest thing you can do is be present in the present…
gratefully."

Maya Angelou

Contents

Introduction

In the autumn of 2016, I joined a business networking group. Most people join networking groups to get clients and business. While that would have been a fantastic benefit for me, it was not my main purpose.

After teaching Tantra and conscious sexuality for twelve years, I felt the Universe guiding me towards something a little different. The whispers and nudges seemed to be telling me to take my skills, tools and practices that I used in the world of sexual healing into the business world. The business world was not one I knew well, if at all. However, once I accepted my mission, things began to unfold in interesting ways — as they always do.

I joined the networking community for two specific, strategic reasons:

1. To talk to and learn from people in business. What were their hopes and fears? What was working for them and what wasn't? How open were they to what I used to refer

to as my 'hippie woo woo' language? I was told off by a business coach for calling what I do 'hippie woo woo'. She reminded me that it is ancient wisdom, and she is right!

2. To start public speaking, specifically to smaller groups that would be warm and friendly and, hopefully, interested. I knew that if I were to accept the full mission, I would need to do more public speaking. Even though I'd facilitated workshops for years and even taught groups of up to seventy to one hundred people, public speaking felt like a different kettle of fish.

I developed my first talk, called "The Number One Most Important Skill for Bedroom and Business". I wanted to bridge the gap between my previous twelve years of experience and the new world I was venturing into.

What do you think the 'Number One Most Important Skill' is? I'll tell you; the number one most important skill for bedroom and business is *presence* — being fully present, right here, right now. Meditation is all about being in the present moment.

The talk was well received, and I enjoyed sharing it with lots of groups around the country.

After giving this talk many times over several months, I felt like it had done its time and I needed a fresh new talk, more in line with the direction in which I was heading. This time I created a talk called 'Leading From The Heart', which was my way of leaning towards talking about Conscious Leadership without using the word 'conscious' yet. Again, this was strategic. I wanted to see if I could introduce and talk about the concept of Conscious Leadership without directly mentioning it. I wanted to see if the concept itself would make sense, because I felt that the term Conscious Leadership might be off-putting or confusing for some people who might otherwise be interested in it.

As I took the talk to different groups around the country, people told me how much it had touched them, that it really resonated with them and that they learned something new and useful from it. My talks are never just me talking. They are always full of audience participation. They are interactive. I know that people learn better when they have an embodied experience of what you're talking about.

In the 'Leading From The Heart', talk there are four or five opportunities for audiences to participate, to learn by doing. Three of these required them to close their eyes and take their awareness or mind's eye inwards for a moment or two or to reflect on something.

The formal structure of these events included free networking time; the twenty-minute talk; and three, ten-minute, one-to-one chats with different people. After one particular talk, I sat down to talk with a lovely man, a travel agent named Guy Johnson. We'd met at previous meetings but hadn't had a one-to-one chat before.

He started to tell me how he'd enjoyed the talk and the exercises we did. He went on to say that he'd recently been trying to meditate, but that he found it difficult to sit still and just empty his mind. He said he couldn't stop thinking, which led him to feel he was not a good meditator and perhaps meditation wasn't for him.

Alarmed, I shared with him that sitting still and emptying your mind is just one of many, many ways to meditate. In fact, I said kind of flippantly, I bet there are at least 101 ways to meditate. I went on to share lots of ways with him. Loads of ways just rolled out of my mind.

I told him that meditation is really just bringing your full attention to whatever is in front of you. Yes, sitting still, in silence, and trying not to have any thoughts is one way, but it most certainly isn't the only way. He was delighted to hear this!

After the meeting I couldn't stop thinking about our conversation. I started thinking about all the people who might have tried this same way and failed, or felt uncomfortable, and so quit.

I was so inspired by this conversation and the thoughts that followed that I did a spontaneous Facebook Live called '101 Ways to Meditate for Business Success'. I scribbled down about forty-five ways and a few other notes and jumped on Facebook.

Although I hadn't announced that I was going to be doing the

Facebook Live event, I had quite a few people tune in and some amazing comments.

Comments included:

- Excellent talk!
- Beautiful truth.
- Resonating a LOT.
- That was really enlightening, thank you.
- I'm saving this video!
- Wise words, Rebecca, every moment becomes a prayer, a meditation. Thank you.
- This is the most sensual spiritual talk I've ever seen. Quite beautiful!

And so the seed of this book was born.

The bottom line of all the work I do, including the sexuality work, is bringing people into the present moment. That is all there is. The past is no longer here and the future never arrives. When it gets here, it is always now.

Becoming aware of the present moment takes practice. We live in a world currently designed to divide our attention and keep us distracted. Learning to be present is a bit like learning to play an instrument or build muscles at the gym. You have to practice regularly. You learn a bit on your own and a bit from others. It gets a little bit easier as you go, except for days when it doesn't.

The process of coming into and being aware of the present moment *is* meditation.

Want to know how meditation can improve your life, your business and your experiences in the bedroom? Read on . . .

How to Use This Book

The best way to use this book is the way that works best for you. Seriously, you know you better than I do. Do what feels right for you.

- You can skim through, see what resonates and choose a meditation (or two) to try straight away.
- You can read it from cover to cover before you get started.
- You can skip all the chapters you don't want to read or that don't resonate with you and just pick and choose the ones that do.
- You can choose one or five or seventeen practices and just do those.
- You can try all of them, in whatever order works for you.
- Take what works for you in this book and leave the rest.

Read through the different suggestions and see which ones jump out at you. Which ones draw you in and make you more curious. Try a few out. See how they feel. You will find some really suit you and your present situation and others may not be for you. Some might seem easier or more relevant, depending on what is going on in your life and in your work or business.

If you try some and they don't resonate with you, don't give up! There are 101 ways suggested here and there are many more. Play around with these. Use them as guidelines rather than as rules.

If I've written something that doesn't work for you or that you feel is wrong, you have a choice. You can decide the whole book is worthless and put it down for good ... or you can keep reading, skimming and see if you can find something that *is* helpful and that *does* add to or enhance your meditation practice.

Even if it's just one new thing or a different way of looking at something, you will have expanded and grown. Hurray!

Chapter 1

What Is Meditation Anyway?

When I started writing this book, I did what many authors do these days. I did some research on Facebook. I posted the following questions in a couple of groups I was in at the time:

What is meditation to you?
What do you think of when someone says they meditate?
What do you think meditation is?

Here are some of the answers I received:

- Time out, quiet thought, relaxation, positive energy.
- Yep, time out. Greater focus as well, not always easy but I'm working on it.
- A spiritual faith connection.
- Different for everyone, there's no right way. Sometimes a gateway to bliss, sometimes a frustrating battle to sit

through it. Something I've done for years but never established an enduring daily practice.

- I meditate 100s of times a day. I just switch off and lose all thought. This could be whilst washing up, cleaning. I also do the guided meditations, where I go very deep, but I have managed now to just switch off at the click of my fingers.
- Bliss.
- Many years ago, meditation was something I perceived of as unnatural, unnecessary and something that would not work on me. I had made a huge amount of assumptions. Until only recently, as I wasn't able to find a "me" moment and I wasn't able to calm down, I tried meditation, despite my negative beliefs. I tried meditation and it truly worked at that precise moment! I cannot say that it has helped me beyond that point but perhaps I need to practice it more consistently.
- I have struggled massively with "traditional" meditation and have instead tried to make my own way of stilling my frenetic brain.

What do you think? Are these answers in line with your own thoughts and experiences of meditation?

Meditation can be all of those things. A time to quiet the mind, get still and refocus. Time out of your busy day or life to recenter and recalibrate. A way to connect to Source or God or the Universe. A way to get quiet and still and slow down the often-overburdened mind. Something that can lead to bliss and relaxation as well as frustration and difficulty.

Many people think that 'proper' meditation is sitting with your legs crossed, spine straight and your eyes closed. Hands lying palm up on your knees or thighs, with forefinger and thumb lightly touching. Ideally, this 'proper' meditation takes place in a quiet room while you try to clear your mind of all thoughts for a set period of time. This *is* one way of meditating. It's a good way of meditating. However, it's not for everyone, and it's definitely not the only way.

This is what I'll refer to as 'Classic Meditation'. Chapter six is all about Classic Meditation.

You can also meditate without sitting down, without being still, and with your eyes open. More on that in a moment.

I love meditating in the classic way. I try to sit for at least fifteen minutes every morning in Classic Meditation pose. I often use this type of meditation when I need to come back to my centre, get focused or grounded. It is a beautiful, calming way to still the body and mind.

Often, I get insights or ideas popping up. Sometimes I feel serene and peaceful. Other times, I feel like I've been travelling in the cosmos, expanding my cells and molecules. I almost always feel more relaxed and present. Occasionally I can't stop thinking about things I have going on or a song that's stuck in my head. That's just the way it is. That's why meditation is called a practice. It's not something to get perfect, ever, just something to continue to practice in the moment.

Let me offer my working definition of meditation here.

Meditation is bringing yourself fully to the present moment.

It is being utterly present to whatever is right in front of you.

Expanded further, meditation is being so fully present and in the moment that everything else falls away and time slows down. It is being so fully engaged that your heart opens, you feel totally connected to Source and bliss is right there in that moment — no matter what you are doing. Thoughts may come and go, but you return to a singular focus.

You practice being present in the moment. That is meditation.

> *"Meditation is pure fascination with this moment, exactly as it is." Jeff Foster*

Since meditation is about being fully present, almost anything can be a meditation if done with intention.

You can be fully present with your breath, with a flower, while dancing, singing, making love or making dinner. More on this later in the book.

When you bring your full presence to whatever you're doing, you are immersed in the present moment, which is all there is. When you bring your full presence to whatever you're doing, life becomes more intimate, more connected. You feel your interconnectedness to life.

As you practice being in the present moment, your body relaxes, your immune system is boosted, your heart rate finds equilibrium and frayed nerve endings are soothed.

As you practice being in the present moment, your mind quiets, your thoughts subside, and peace and contentment arise.

You now have access to Source energy, deep wisdom and Infinite Intelligence.

Source energy is also known as the Universe, Higher Power, Divinity, God, Cosmic Energy, the 'All-That-Is' or Universal Consciousness. It is the vast, unlimited wisdom, energy and unconditional love that is the very core of everything in existence.

When I was doing research for this book, I read that there have been at least 3000 scientific studies into the health benefits of meditation. Apart from the fact that cultures all over the world have diverse systems of meditation going back millennia, modern scientists have now proven that it is good for you. Here are just some of the benefits:

- Reduces stress and anxiety
- Increases wholeheartedness, compassion and empathy
- Opens creative channels
- Increases self-awareness
- Greatly improves health
- Improves concentration and focus

- Boosts confidence and self-esteem
- Improves sleep
- Boosts physical, mental, emotional and spiritual health
- Deepens self-awareness
- Increases cognitive retention
- Enhances mood
- Improves performance and efficiency
- Improves memory
- Slows ageing

This list is really just a beginning. Everyone who meditates regularly will have their own unique experiences and lists of benefits. I'll share some of those stories with you later in the book.

Let's take a closer look now at how meditation or being fully present can benefit you in your life, business and the bedroom.

Chapter 2

What Does Success
Mean in This Context?

This book would be remiss if it didn't take a minute to talk about success and what that means in this context.

What does success in life, business and the bedroom really look like?

What are we aiming for?

Does there need to be a place, i.e. 'success', to get to, and how will we know if we've gotten there?

On one level, 'success' is when we feel we've achieved something or reached a predetermined goal. We feel good when we feel like we've achieved something. We're hardwired for that.

This sort of success is often action based. It's often about 'doing' and 'getting'. It might mean having money, getting a promotion or owning the latest car or shoes.

What looks and feels like success at this level will be different from one person to another.

So what does it mean in the context of this book?

We are constantly bombarded with ideas and images of what success is or should be. If our ideas of success are different or we don't reach someone else's idea of success, we feel like a failure or not good enough.

Doesn't make sense, does it? Doesn't seem like a good, self-loving, productive way to live.

Looking a little deeper, we might define success as whatever feels like achievement to your heart and soul.

This isn't about conventional, egoic success. This is about success that touches that deeper, inner part of you. Not the part that wants to win so it looks good to others, but the bit that is truly nourished by achieving something that's meaningful to *you*, regardless of what anyone else thinks.

This sort of success might mean growing flowers or vegetables in your garden, making time to read, paint or cook, or finally signing up for that course you've been wanting to take.

These still require some action, but go beyond the conventional layer of success. These nurture you on a deeper level.

Looking deeper still, we might define success as just being fully present and in the moment. No action, no doing. There is nowhere to get to.

This sort of success isn't something that's 'over there' or will happen one day. This sort of success is available to you in each moment. Just like each moment is an opportunity to meditate, i.e. be present, so each moment is an opportunity for success.

What if just allowing yourself to feel what was present equalled success?

What if just taking one conscious breath equalled success?

How about this for a working definition of success in the context of this book: success is being present, even for a moment, with what is right here, right now. Success is being present. Success is BEing.

Take a moment to reflect on the different layers of success and what success means to you. It's absolutely okay to have longer-term goals of success! It's okay to have conventional goals of success. However, also reflect on what success looks like to you today. This morning. In this moment right now. How can you set yourself up to win in each moment?

Important note: be careful to not fall into the trap of thinking that success = feeling good.

While feeling good is certainly a great goal, a lot of people override or suppress their true feelings to appear as if they're 'feeling good'. To somehow trick themselves and others into thinking everything is 'fine' (said through gritted teeth).

We've been led to believe that there are good and bad feelings. Sure, we might have a preference to not feel sad or angry, but those feelings are not intrinsically bad. They are energy in motion.

Emotion = energy in motion

Rather than focusing on 'feeling good' as a measurè of success or successful meditation, how about focusing on feeling and allowing whatever is arising?

Chapter 3

How Will Meditation Help Me in
Life, Business and the Bedroom?

Have you ever seen the film *Click* with Adam Sandler? In the film, Adam plays a man who finds a magical remote control. It allows him to click through the parts of his life that are painful, difficult or just annoying. He clicks through arguments with his wife, through things he considers boring or insignificant, and finally, through the death of his father. At the end of the film, he realises that by doing that, he's missed all the parts that make life juicy, meaningful and connected. He's missed out on intimacy with life.

Meditation, however you practice it, brings you into intimacy with life. It gives you the full-flavoured, high-res, Technicolor, surround sound version of life.

A really important part of meditation is the context of your life. How your life is in your twenties is obviously very different to your life in your thirties, forties, fifties, and so on. Each decade brings its own opportunity for growth, learning and expansion. New possibilities open up to us as we move through the stages of life.

Meditation helps you to keep coming back to yourself during these transitions. It helps you stay true to yourself. To be in alignment with your truth, your values and your purpose.

In fact, you could say that meditation is an ancient technology for just that. Keeping you connected to who-you-really-are, beyond just your name and job title, which has nothing at all to do with who-you-really-are.

Let's talk in practical terms, shall we?

What will a regular meditation practice do for you?

What is the one thing that is at the very centre, the very core of your life, your relationships and your work or business? No matter who you are in love with or what job you're doing? No matter where you're living or what your financial situation is? That one thing is *you*.

You are the foundation on which your life is built. You are the core from which your life experiences emerge. Even if you don't believe that, and you feel that things happen *to* you rather than *from* you, you are still central to the story of your life. As such, *you* are the only thing you really ever have control over. Even if you believe you can't control what happens to you, you *can* control how you respond. Well, you can learn to. It's a practice. And that's where meditation comes in.

Meditation practised regularly gives you a sanctuary, a safe place, a home base, as it were. It's a way to return to your core self, your foundation, your centeredness.

How Will It Help Me in Life?

"Meditation practice isn't about trying to throw ourselves away and become something better, it's about befriending who we are." Ani Pema Chodron

Any time you come into the present moment, your life is improved.

Life is only ever happening in the present moment. The past has gone and when the future arrives, it's always now.

We live in a world that is chock-full of distractions. We can access information from all over the world in a fraction of a second. We are in contact with more people at once than ever before.

"We are living in a culture entirely hypnotized by the illusion of time, in which the so-called present moment is felt as nothing but an infinitesimal hairline between an all-powerfully causative past and

an absorbingly important future. We have no present. Our consciousness is almost completely preoccupied with memory and expectation. We do not realize that there never was, is, nor will be any other experience than present experience. We are therefore out of touch with reality." Alan Watts

It's easy to lose yourself when so much is being demanded of you. When your attention is constantly being required outside of yourself.

Having a practice to bring you back to yourself, back to the present moment, keeps you grounded and in alignment with 'who-you-really-are'.

Recently, science has caught up with what Eastern mystics have been saying for centuries — that there are very real, tangible benefits to having a regular meditation practice.

On the physical level, meditation can reduce stress, lower your heart rate, boost your immune system and calm the nervous system. On the mental/emotional level, regular meditation can increase happiness and resilience, increase your ability to connect with yourself and others, and also boost overall confidence. Over time, it can also increase creativity, problem-solving and decision-making.

How Will Meditation Help Me in Business?

"My life is better when I get still regularly. Call it meditation or call it quiet time — doesn't matter. The benefits are the same. If you stay with the practice, it's like developing spiritual muscle. I promise you will become less stressed, more focused."
Oprah Winfrey

Meditation for business success? Really?

Yes, really.

Whether you work for yourself or are employed by someone else, the way we do business is changing. The old way was very ego-centred. Success was measured by how much money and power over others you had.

The emerging way of business is much more heart lead. It's more compassionate, people-centred and mindful.

Why?

Because the world is changing. As technology expands and more tasks become automated or machine driven, people have to focus on what people do better than technology. We have to be more creative, empathic and relational in our work.

Also, humanity as a whole is evolving. When we swing too far one way, we always come back around for balance. Ultimately, money and 'power over' are not fulfilling. Not on a deeper soul level. The old way isn't and never was sustainable.

As humanity evolves, the desire to be more connected and more in alignment is showing up even in business.

Jeff Weiner, the CEO of LinkedIn, has been on Oprah's *Super Soul Sunday* talking about what he calls Compassionate Leadership, and how it's changed him as a leader and the culture at LinkedIn for the better.

Big business entrepreneurs and leaders are talking about self-awareness, empathy, and even presence in terms of business. More and more companies have wellness and mindfulness programs.

The old business way was to bring your 'business self' to work. Leave your life outside of work at the door, put on your corporate facade and proceed with your day. Hide the best parts of yourself — the parts that make you YOU, that make you unique and fun and shiny, and put on an 'appropriate for work' mask.

This hiding of who you really are increases stress and illness. It leads to feeling that who we are is not enough, not valuable, not wanted. It also puts up a barrier between you and others. This might be your colleagues or clients and customers. It reduces intimacy and trust.

However, we need these to create a healthy, positive working environment. One which encourages growth (both of its employees and of the business itself), transformation, creativity and innovation. We actually need to bring our full self to work for the business to thrive.

Fortunately, this old way, this old structure or paradigm, is dying away.

> *"Extraordinary things begin to happen when we dare to bring all of who we are to work'. Frederic Laloux, author of Reinventing Organisations.*

Nowadays, business leaders, even in large corporates, are using terms like 'mindfulness' and 'well-being'.

The prolific writer, speaker and entrepreneur Gary Vaynerchuk talks repeatedly about the importance of self-awareness and empathy in business and in leadership. Arianna Huffington of the *Huffington Post* started a whole new movement called Thrive (about thriving rather than surviving) and is promoting self-care and getting plenty of good sleep.

At the core of this new emerging paradigm is the requirement that we know ourselves on deeper levels. We need to know what we value, what gives us a sense of purpose, what we enjoy and what we won't tolerate any more.

This new paradigm requires much greater self-awareness than ever before. Self-awareness is when you really know yourself. You know and own your strengths and play to them. You know and accept your weaknesses, and you still deeply love yourself. Self-awareness requires you to be willing to be seen, to be vulnerable, and to be accountable for your mistakes.

This new paradigm requires us to be aware of our connection to ourselves, to each other and to the world at large.

Meditation gives us a way to cultivate and experience these connections.

The various meditations that are offered in this book give you ways to connect. To connect to the present moment. To yourself. To your partner, your colleagues, to nature and so forth.

In this new business paradigm, it is crucial that you are able to connect. Being able to connect is very different to what was required of you in the old paradigm. Now you are being asked to be seen instead of hiding, to engage rather than play small, to bring all of yourself instead of the 'work self'.

Here are some of the benefits that relate directly to business:

- Reduced stress and anxiety
- Increased resilience and ability to cope with pressure
- Better intuition and access to creative solutions
- Better decision making
- Improved memory

- Expanded attention span
- Better focus and concentration
- Increased clarity and vision
- Better overall health
- Enhanced cognitive skills

How Will Meditation Help Me in the Bedroom?

I've had the honour and pleasure of working as a sexuality teacher, healer and practitioner for over twelve years.

For years, I received emails and phone calls from people asking if I could them teach 'methods and techniques' for being a better lover. My answer was always, 'Well, yes and no. I could teach you all the methods and techniques in the world, but none of them will matter if you don't first master the most important part of intimacy, pleasure and connection. And once you've mastered that, you don't really need "methods and techniques."'

So what's the secret? What's the most important part of intimacy, pleasure and connection?

Presence.

Being fully, totally, 100 percent present — in your body, in the moment, with your lover — whether that's in the bedroom or with nature, washing the dishes or whatever you are doing. Sexuality, intimacy and pleasure are about so much more than sex!

Presence is where intimacy lives. Without presence, there is no intimacy. Without intimacy, you are just going through the motions. That's true in the bedroom and in life in general.

My number one tip for being an amazing lover, enjoying sex, intimacy and pleasure? Learn to be present. That is just what meditation teaches you to do.

Chapter 4

Preparing to Meditate

"You should meditate for twenty minutes a day unless you're too busy; then you should sit for an hour." Old Zen saying

As you will see as you read through the meditations in this book, a few of them are more formal and might need a bit of preparation, while most of them are very laid-back and can happen spontaneously in the moment.

For most of the meditations, hopefully you will at least switch off your phone or put it on silent or airplane mode. Put down your laptop, iPad, and other technology. Take off your watch and your shoes where possible. Turn off the telly and any distractions.

Obviously, if you are listening to music, a guided meditation, setting a timer or maybe even using a meditation app, then you will need to access it via a phone or other technology. That's okay, just be sure to switch off notifications.

You want as few interruptions as possible.

That said, as already mentioned, meditation is really just being fully present to what is. So if distractions happen, rather than getting upset, rattled or thinking it's all ruined, you have two choices.

You can notice the 'interruption' and return to your meditation, return your awareness to what you were doing or focusing on before.

Or you can just gently switch your presence to the new thing, the thing that 'interrupted' you. Practice being open and curious and see what happens.

The Symphony of Life

Many years ago, I attended an energy healing course. It took place above a shop in St Albans. The shop was in the town centre and at weekends, there was a lively market just outside.

We had the window open and could just about hear the bustling crowd outside. That in itself wasn't too intrusive. Then right around lunchtime, we could hear the sound of metal scraping on metal. Over and over again. Turned out to be a stall, right below our window, selling Chinese food. The sound was the chef cooking food in a wok.

We were being led through a series of guided meditations at the time. A couple of people asked the teacher to shut the window because they found the new noise a distraction. They were noticeably annoyed.

To my surprise, she refused. She said it was all a part of the great symphony of life and that our practice was to stay present with what we were doing. They weren't too pleased, but I was delighted!

It taught me a huge lesson. I didn't need to change anything outside of myself for the moment to be okay. I just had to keep returning my awareness, my presence, my focus, to where I wanted it.

Chapter 5

Breath

Breathing is one of those things we usually take for granted. We don't have to think about it or control it. We don't even have to know how it works. Breathing is always happening while we're going about our lives, doing our work, driving, making love, and even when we're sleeping.

When you are breathing on autopilot, it's the primal part of the brain, the brainstem, that does the work. The brainstem regulates basic life functions, ones that happen without conscious thought. These include heart rate and blood pressure, digestion, swallowing, reflexive actions such as sneezing or coughing, as well as temperature, levels of alertness, sense of balance, and ability to sleep.

When we consciously control our breath, we move from the brainstem to the cerebrum, the more modern part of the brain. The more conscious part.

The cerebrum has many functions and subfunctions, however, as a whole, it is responsible for voluntary actions as well as thinking and reasoning, language and speech, hearing, visuals, planning and conscious thought.

It is from the more conscious part of our brains that we can change our minds, change our thinking, change our perspective and change our lives. We go from living by default to living by choice. We live less from the animal impulse part and more from the ever-growing and evolving conscious being part. This gives us power over our lives, how we live them, and how we respond to people, events and situations around us. All it takes is one conscious breath.

Learning to use your breath fully and properly is a whole technology, an ancient technology. There are whole books, practices and methods for using your breath to change your body, mind and soul.

Your every in-breath is a commitment to living, no matter how tough your life might be in this moment. Your every out-breath is an act of trust. Trust that the next moment will bring more life-giving breath.

You can use breath to move and release energy and emotions that are stuck in the body, to improve digestion and to improve sleep.

You can use your breath consciously to relax deeply, lower blood pressure, reduce stress, and cultivate calmness, clarity and focus at work.

You can also use it to connect with a lover, to direct sexual energy, to get better erections, last longer in bed, and to create multiple, full-bodied and mind-blowing orgasms.

Conscious breathing brings you into the present moment. Your breath is always in the present moment, and when you are consciously aware of it, so are you.

The First, Most Simple Meditation

If you only ever do one meditation from this book, make it this one.

1. Notice that you're breathing

There are many, many breathing techniques for meditation, health and healing. Let's start with the simplest one. Focusing on your breath is the quickest, easiest way to come into the present moment. Your breath is always right here, right now. It can't be in the past, and when the future gets here, it's the present.

All you have to do is pause for a moment and notice that you're breathing.

Notice your in-breath and notice your out-breath.

You don't have to change anything or breathe in any special way.

As you focus on your breath, you are in the present moment. Your breath can only ever be in the present moment. When you are consciously aware of it, so are you.

You can do this with your eyes open or closed. Do it for just a moment or two or for an extended period, whatever feels right at the time.

Chapter 6

Getting Started with Classic Meditations

As mentioned previously, I'm using the term Classic Meditation here to refer to the 'sitting cross-legged, hands resting palm upwards on thighs, spine straight, eyes closed, clear your thoughts' kind of meditating.

It is a fantastic, deep way to meditate.

I was introduced to this form of meditation in a Tantra workshop years ago. At the time, I didn't really know much about meditation or how to do it.

I didn't understand how this form of meditation would help me know myself more deeply, or how it would positively impact my connection to my sexuality, my sexual self and my relationships.

Turns out the teacher knew a thing or two.

She had learned meditation while living with Osho (a modern, controversial mystic credited with bringing Tantra to the west) in Pune. She told us a story about learning to meditate there.

She said that they were expected to sit in classic meditation pose for forty minutes, or longer, every day. They sat outside in the baking hot sun. Usually, there were flies buzzing around their faces and sweat pouring down their brows.

They were instructed to sit still and quiet and not move at all. When they experienced discomfort in the body from sitting or flies buzzing around their faces, they were to just notice it, but not move to correct it.

She said that more often than not, the urge to move or swat a fly away or scratch an itch would eventually just fade away. It was the mind playing tricks, trying to distract you from your meditation. She said that if that happened to us, we were to just notice what our minds were doing as if watching a child at play.

At that time, I was experiencing some backache and knee problems. I was convinced that there was no way I'd be able to sit in classic position, unsupported, for forty minutes. I was pretty sure I'd be in agony by the time it was all over, *and* I was also up for the challenge.

After explaining it all, she gave us a couple of minutes to get settled and told us she'd ring a bell to signify the beginning and again when we were finished. There were about seventy of us in the room. There was lots of shuffling and sniffling and coughing, but eventually, everyone settled down.

I followed my breath for a while and then, just as expected, thoughts of discomfort started to appear. My back and then my knees started their usual protest.

To the best of my ability at that time, I practised just noticing the thoughts that were arising. Rather than attach to the thoughts, I witnessed them lovingly. I didn't move or try to change anything other than how I perceived what was going on. I knew my mind was trying to get my attention. Instead, I stayed present with my body and my breath.

Surprisingly, the aches soon drifted off.

Like my physical aches, my awareness drifted in and out of being fully present, to what felt like floating in the cosmic soup, to watching my thoughts, to feeling bored and wondering when it would be over and how on earth I was going to make it to the end.

Much sooner than I'd anticipated, the bell rang. We were finished. It was wonderful and perplexing at the same time. I was so pleased to have managed it. There were no aches or pains in my body — no new ones anyway. I felt a deeper inner peace than ever before and didn't beat myself up for the times my mind wandered.

It was quite the revelation.

I had had an embodied experience of how disconnecting from the mind, stilling the body and being present with breath could facilitate inner knowing, deeper connection and more self-awareness.

It's important to point out here that we had been doing some deep personal and energetic work in the two or three days leading up to this meditation experience. If we'd started with that straight off the bat, I might have had a very different experience. Plus, meditating in a group that is being professionally guided and held is different than meditating on your own. Not better, just different.

Meditation, however you do it, is always different. Some days it works better than others. Some days it is profound and life-changing. Other days not much happens, or you feel bored. Don't compare your experiences to mine or anyone else's. There is one more story to share from this teacher.

While living in Pune with Osho, my teacher and the other students would have weekly meetings with Osho himself. My teacher had been given the assignment to learn to meditate in such a way that she became one with the Oneness (Universe, divinity, cosmos, god, love — use whatever word feels right to you here). For weeks she would attend her personal session with Osho, show him how she'd got on, and for weeks he would tell her no, she hadn't quite managed it yet.

Eventually, she felt she'd accomplished what had been asked of her. Excited to share this with her teacher, she made her way to her weekly appointment.

She sat down in front of him and began to meditate. Once she'd hit that magical place, soaring in the cosmic Oneness, Osho whispered to her, 'That's great, now come back'.

This wasn't the response she'd been expecting at all. Instead, she'd expected him to applaud her efforts, to congratulate her, to tell her to stay in the Oneness, floating for eternity.

The real lesson, it turned out, was to access the Oneness and then bring your 'knowingness' of it, your experience of it, into your everyday life. To live your present, earthly, embodied life while connected to Source/Oneness.

Ultimately, that's what meditation is about. Being so fully present in each moment that each moment becomes an experience of Oneness.

Simple Classic Meditations

For each of these meditations, find somewhere safe and comfortable to sit. You can sit on a chair or you can sit cross-legged on the floor or on a cushion. Have your spine straight and relaxed if you can.

You can also do these in whatever way suits your body best. The most important thing is your intention and remembering to breathe.

Once you are comfortable and settled, choose one of the following meditations to begin with. Set a timer for five to ten minutes for your first time. You can do one meditation repeatedly for a week or longer, or you can try a new one each day. Trust your intuition, your inner 'spidey senses', and your body's wisdom. Be open to whatever happens.

As you get more comfortable with this form of meditation, you can extend the length of time you sit if you wish.

Begin all of the Classic Meditation practices below with this:

Sit comfortably, close your eyes and relax your body. Allow your hips, shoulders, spine and neck to relax. Relax the muscles of your face and jaw. Take a long, slow, deep breath in through your nose and then breathe out through your mouth, long and slow, allowing a sighing sound. Relax your body even more. Allow your breathing to return to normal. Then try one of the practices below.

2. One deep breath

Take a long, s l o w, deep breath in through your nose. Really fill up your lungs. Then slowly and gently breathe out through your nose, slower than you think you can. Allow your body, especially your shoulders and jaw, to relax fully as you breathe out.

With that one conscious breath, you have moved from the primal brain to the modern brain. You have stimulated the conscious, thinking part of the brain. You have moved from the past to the present.

It really is that simple.

This 'technique' works for life, business and the bedroom. It works every day in just about every situation.

3. Notice the spaces

While there are many benefits to following your in-breaths and out-breaths, there are also benefits to becoming aware of the spaces between your breaths.

Become aware of your breath. Don't change it in any way, just become aware that you are breathing in and breathing out.

After a moment or two, become aware that there is a space in between the in-breath and out-breath, as well as between the out-breath and the in-breath.

Observe these spaces for a while without moving to change them.

Gently allow the spaces to expand a bit. Allow a slightly longer pause between each breath. How does that feel?

As you practice this and become more and more aware of the natural spaces in your breathing, you are better able to be aware of the spaces between your thoughts.

Over time, you begin to realise or experience that you are not your thoughts, but really the space in which thoughts arise. There is a deep well of peace and calm at the centre of you.

Focusing on the spaces in your breath will guide you to that well.

4. Repeat a specific chosen word or phrase

Sometimes it can be really difficult to get the mind to quieten down. Not just during meditation, but throughout the day. What I find most useful then is to give the mind something to do.

In this instance, you're going to repeat a specific chosen word or phrase over and over.

A really simple one is to internally narrate your breathing pattern. Like this: I'm breathing in, I'm breathing out, I'm breathing in, I'm breathing out... Sounds a bit simple and maybe mundane, but it's amazing how helpful it is. Your body and soul can get on with relaxing while you are present to what's occurring with your breath. A win-win situation!

Other things you might repeat include:

- I am at peace.
- I am rested, calm and happy.
- I am present.
- I love and trust my body.
- I am love.
- All is well in my world.

Obviously, you can create your own too. Keep them short and simple. Repeat them silently to yourself. Sometimes when you're doing this, a new thought will arise, and if it feels right, change over to that one. If it doesn't feel right or just feels like a distraction, just notice it and keep going with your original chosen word or phrase.

5. Breathing 4 x 4

Breathe in for a slow count of four

Hold for a slow count of four

Breathe out for a slow count of four

Hold for a slow count of four

If you are skilled at breathing techniques or just feel longer would be right for you, then you can do counts of five or six.

6. Breathe in love, breathe out gratitude

You can do this pretty much anywhere that you can take a moment or two to focus inwardly. Do it as a full meditation or just a few breaths on the train or on your way to a meeting. It will almost instantly shift your vibration and give you a lift.

Allow your natural breathing pace to deepen. Take longer breaths in and exhale gently and fully. Imagine that you are breathing in love. Unconditional, Universal love. It is in abundant, infinite supply and you only have to intend it for it to work.

Then intend to exhale gratitude. You don't even have to pinpoint what you are grateful for with this. Just imagine you are breathing out gratitude.

Do at least two or three breaths or for as long as it feels good.

7. Clearing your body and energy system

This is a great way to give your body and energy system a bit of a clear out. Using your intention and breath, you can energetically draw 'what no longer serves you' up through your body and release it on the out-breath.

Before you begin, imagine that you have a cylinder or pipe that runs from the base of your body, up through the middle or trunk, in front of your spine, all the way up to the top of your head.

Set your intention to clear and release anything which no longer serves you. You can say your intention out loud or just internally. You don't need to know exactly what is clearing. Your body and energy system have their own intelligence. Trust them to do this clearing for you.

Taking long, slow, deep breaths, use your in-breath to draw 'what no longer serves you' up from your base, all the way through the pipe or channel, to the top of your head. On your out-breath, release it all through the top of your head.

If visualisation helps you, you might like to imagine a water fountain, fireworks or even the spray a whale makes.

What happens to the 'stuff' you are releasing? Well, just as the earth turns manure into fertilizer and grows beautiful flowers, whatever you release is transformed too. My experience is that it is instantly transformed into sparkly light or effervescent energy.

You can do a few of these as and when you need them or as part of a regular practice.

8. Getting grounded

There are a couple of ways you can do this one. If you are sitting, imagine your roots growing down from your base. If you are standing, then imagine them growing from your feet. You can do both if that feels right to you.

Get yourself comfortable and relax your body. Imagine you have roots growing down from your base or feet into the earth. Allow them to grow deep and wide. Allow the roots themselves to grow thicker and to reach further down.

Imagine them going deep down through the layers of the earth. Once you feel they've gone as deep as they need to in that moment, become aware of how safe and secure you are. Become aware of how firm your foundations are. Notice how good it feels to be rooted, grounded.

Allow rich, earthy energy and nutrients to travel up the roots to your body and energy system.

Open your body, heart and soul and drink in as much as you need.

Allow feelings of safety and security, groundedness, belonging and deep holding to travel up the roots. Know that you are safe, held and nourished.

These are also magical roots. They don't hold you in one place, they travel with you wherever you go.

After you've practised this a few times, it becomes easier and quicker to tap into the feeling of being grounded. So rather than needing to do a whole meditation, you can just tune in to the feeling that is already there, albeit in the background.

You can go about your day feeling grounded, rooted, safe and secure, as well as nourished and taken care of.

9. Connecting to Source

Relax your body and focus on your breath for a moment. Use your awareness or mind's eye to trace the outline of your body. Get a sense of the edges of your physical self. Take a few deep breaths.

Now expand your awareness out to the energy field surrounding your body, still in the shape of your physical self. Imagine that you are more than just your physical body.

Take your awareness to the top of your head. Notice the energy field just above the top of your head. You might feel a warmth or tingling sensation or like your head is expanding, and it's okay if you don't.

Imagine this area to be a sort of portal or opening. A place through which Universal, cosmic energy can travel for your highest good. Use your imagination and see how it feels.

Now take your awareness out into the cosmos. Imagine going past the planets and stars, farther than you've imagined before.

Keep going until you get a sense of what I call Source, Cosmic Energy or Infinite Intelligence. You might feel the energy suddenly shift or get lighter and clearer. You might feel a slight tingle or twinkling sensation. You might just intuitively know you're where you need to be.

Now imagine using your in-breaths to draw this energy down and into the top of your head. Sort of like drinking it through a straw — down from the cosmos and into your heart.

Release this energy into your heart on the out-breath.

Another way to do this is to visualise that cosmic energy is pouring down a funnel into the top of your head and into your heart. Try both ways and see what feels right to you.

When your heart feels full you can either stop there or continue to fill up your whole body. Allow that cosmic energy to fill you up so fully that it seeps out of your pores and drips out of your fingertips.

10. Connecting to Earth and Source at the same time

This one takes a minute to get your head around, but once you get it, feels great.

Relax your body fully and allow your breath to deepen.

Start to draw earth energy upwards on your in-breaths. Imagine rich, earthy energy travelling up and in through the soles of your feet or your base, all the way up to your heart. On your out-breath, release this earthy energy directly into your heart.

Do this three or four times.

Then let that go and shift your focus to drawing down Source energy on your in-breath. Draw it down through the top of your head and into your heart. Release this Source energy into your heart on the out-breath.

Do this three or four times.

Now you're ready to combine both breaths.

On your in-breath, imagine drawing earth energy up into your heart and Source energy down into your heart at the same time. Release both into your heart on the out-breath.

Do this three or four times, or until you feel like stopping.

11. Tuning into and breathing in qualities and characteristics

A really beautiful way to meditate is to focus on a particular quality that you'd like to connect with or draw into your life.

You can do this as part of a Classic Meditation, as you're falling asleep, before an important meeting or any other way that feels right to you.

Qualities and characteristics have unique energy vibrations. These vibrations are always available; you just have to align yourself with that particular energy in order to experience it.

It's a bit like when you tune your radio into your favourite station. The station is always broadcasting its material, its unique energy vibration, and it's up to you to find the right frequency to hear it.

As you adjust the radio dial, you may hear other broadcasts, some more clearly than others. Eventually, you find the station (or vibration) you want, and it comes in loud and clear.

Choose a quality that you'd like to experience, explore, feel, sense or bring into your life.

Say you wanted to feel *gratitude*. Take a few moments to relax, focus on your breathing, and come fully and consciously into the here and now. Then imagine tuning in to the vibration or energy of *gratitude*.

If you're not sure how to do this, try these:

- Instruct or invite your energy system to find the vibration or feeling of *gratitude*.
- Set the intention to align with the vibration of *gratitude*.
- Repeat the word to yourself, '*Gratitude, gratitude, gratitude…*'
- Imagine, visualise or get a sense of a magic dial that you can turn with your mind. Turn the dial to your chosen quality.
- Imagine the quality gently surrounding you, embracing you.
- Imagine it emanating from your body. Where do you feel it in your body?
- Imagine it pouring into you from the Universe.

You know when you've found the right radio station by what you hear. You know you've found the right energy vibration by how you feel.

If you're not sure what the quality you want to focus on feels like, imagine it. Imagine what it *might* feel like. Use your body rather than your mind. Ask your body to show you what it feels like, and then stay tuned in to your body.

Here are some qualities you might like to try to begin with:

Courage

Wholeheartedness

Awe and wonder

Love

Joy

Gratitude

Freedom/Liberty

Delight

Sexual empowerment

Kindness

Trust

Humour

Creativity

Sassiness

Authenticity

Compassion

Contentment

Peacefulness

Boldness

Wisdom

Confidence

Tenderness

Power/Strength

Integrity

Optimism

Sensuality

Empathy

Pleasure

12. Breathing love in and out of the heart

Relax your body and bring your awareness or mind's eye to your heart centre. This includes your actual heart, but is located more in the centre of your chest. Physically, it includes your heart, lungs, thymus gland and some ribs. Metaphysically speaking, it is the area of love, compassion and empathy — for yourself and others.

Start to take longer, slower, deeper breaths.

As you breathe in, intend to breathe in Universal, unconditional love from all directions around you.

As you breathe out, send Universal, unconditional love back out to the Universe, in all directions around you.

Do this for at least three to six breaths, longer if possible.
After a while, if you feel like it, you can direct the love you're breathing out to specific individuals, parts of nature you love or have a connection with, situations in the world, countries, and so on.

Always draw Universal, unconditional love from the Universe and send the same back out.

Send it as an offering, not a demand. Don't push it on anyone or anything. Imagine it arriving at their door and they can choose whether to draw it in or not. Send it from your heart, not your ego. It may or may not be received on the other end. Don't worry about that. Your practice is to allow it to move through you.

13. Gratitude breaths

Thinking, feeling or saying gratitudes is one of the quickest ways to shift and raise your energy. Gratitude brings you into alignment with your true self, your beautiful soul — the one underneath all the conditioning, habits, patterns and fears you've accumulated over your life. These things usually hide or obscure your true self. Gratitude helps shake them off and returns you to yourself.

Take a long, slow, deep breath. As you breathe in, think of something you are grateful for. In your mind, say something like, "I'm grateful for my breath". As you breathe out, imagine that gratitude spreading through your whole body. You can say the same phrase repeatedly or a different one each time.

- I'm grateful for my breath.
- I'm grateful for this day.
- I'm grateful for indoor plumbing.
- I'm grateful for the cup of tea I just had.
- I'm grateful I have food to eat.
- I'm grateful for my body.

See what arises naturally as you meditate.

Chapter 7

Meditations for Life Success

Bringing your full attention, your full presence to anything you do is a form of meditation. The following suggestions are to get you started. Pick and choose the ones that feel right to you. Chop and change them; adapt them to your life and what works for you.

14. Washing up

Absolutely anything can become a meditation if you bring your full awareness to it. Activities you previously complained about or found mundane can become sacred, even ecstatic in nature.

In most situations, you get to choose how you experience whatever is going on. Most of the time you will have the experience you decide to have, or that conditioning has taught you to have.

Rather than spending your precious life complaining or wishing you were doing something else, why not try to fall in love with each moment as it is? Why not consciously choose how you want to experience this moment?

I know, I know — it's a practice, and it's easier on some days than others. Still, what have you got to lose?

In this way, even the washing up is a beautiful opportunity to meditate and be present.

Bring your full attention and awareness to the act and actions of washing up. Open your heart and allow gratitude to flow down your arms and into your hands. Handle the dishes with love and care. Be present to the feel of the water on your hands and the magic of the bubbles of the washing up liquid. Allow gratitude to flow from your heart, and if it feels right, say the words of gratitude out loud.

Here are some suggestions:

- I am grateful for these dishes.
- I am grateful for the food I've just eaten.
- I'm grateful for the opportunity to feed my family.
- I'm grateful to all the people who contributed to getting the food to my home.
- I'm grateful for the water to wash these dishes.
- I'm grateful for the washing up liquid that cleans these dishes.
- I'm grateful for the opportunity to serve my family with love.
- I'm grateful for the sound of the water.

15-18. Walking meditations

Walking meditations are a wonderful way to practice being present. There are several ways to focus your attention while you are walking. Here are some suggestions:

15. Walk slowly, with purpose and intent

Bring your awareness, your attention or your mind's eye to your feet, particularly the soles of your feet. Focus on the movement of your foot, how your heel touches the ground first, the roll of your foot as the ball touches down and then your toes.

Notice how your weight moves from one part of your foot to another.

Notice how your whole body knows intuitively how to balance.

Remember to breathe.

16. Walk barefoot on grass or earth

Otherwise known as 'grounding' or 'earthing', walking barefoot on the earth has been scientifically proven to have extraordinary health benefits. Long before humans put shoes on our feet, we walked sole to earth. It's believed that direct contact can positively impact everything from metabolism to pain reduction.

I often practice walking barefoot and can tell you that I sleep better, my stress almost instantly lowers and I feel healthier — not just in body, but mind and soul too.

Although you can just walk barefoot and still feel the effects, why not do it as a meditation? That added presence and awareness will multiply the benefits.

Find someplace safe to walk barefoot or to just sit with your bare feet touching the ground.

Pay attention to how it feels on your feet first. What temperature, texture and sensations you are experiencing?

Can you feel earth energy moving up your legs?

Can you feel rebalancing happening elsewhere in your body?

Try it for at least ten minutes at a time and see what it does for you.

17. Walk love or gratitude into the earth

"Walk as if you are kissing the Earth with your feet."
Thich Nhat Hanh

Take a minute or two before you set off on your walk to open your heart and tune into the energy and feeling of love or gratitude.

Allow that energy to flow down your body, down your legs, through the soles of your feet and into the earth.

Think of it as walking a blessing from your heart into the earth.

18. Awaken your senses walk

You can do this walk on a city street, in a park or anywhere you happen to be.

Walk slowly and bring your attention to one sense at a time.

For instance, start with sound. Walk for a few minutes, just noticing every single sound you can hear. Do this without preference or judgement. Just be with whatever sounds occur.

After a few minutes, become aware of sensations on your skin. Can you feel warm sunshine, a cool breeze, raindrops?

Then become aware of smell. What can you smell as you continue your walk?

Eventually, focus on sight. What colours and textures can you see? If you look with fresh eyes, as if you've never walked in this place before, what might you notice?

19. Movement or dance

This is a great way to get into your body, to get grounded, and to shift stuck energy.

Don't worry too much about it looking or feeling like proper dancing. The idea is to bring your full attention to your movement, to your body as it moves.

You can do this on your own, with your partner, with your kids or even with your work colleagues! Just a couple of minutes is enough to make a difference.
Try to make it through one whole song if you can. If you've got the time and inclination, carry on for as long as you wish.

Have a boogie in the shower or over breakfast. Get your wiggle on before a lecture or interview. If you sit still for long parts of the day, get up and shake, shimmy and strut your stuff every thirty to forty-five minutes, or as you feel the need.

Choose a piece of music that suits how you'd like to move. It can be rock and roll, classical, heavy metal or whatever you're in the mood for.

Bring all of your attention and awareness to your body and to however you're feeling. Slowly but surely allow your body to start moving.

Don't have a preconceived idea of how you're going to move.

Don't try to move to the music exactly. Pay more attention to your body and emotions and how they want to dance together.

How do they want to move? What wants to be expressed? How does your body naturally express your 'you-ness'? How does it move if you allow your emotions to flow through?

Focus on your body or on the intimate edges where the music is moving your body like a dance partner leading the dance. Allow emotions to flow if they come up. Make sure to ground yourself and drink some water afterwards.

20. Eye-gaze with nature

Eye-gazing is a beautifully deep practice of being utterly present with your eyes. It's not staring, but rather allowing a soft gaze with a person, a tree, a flower, or anything at all. We'll talk more about doing this with a person in the Bedroom section. For now, practice doing this with something out in nature or even a houseplant.

Active Versus Receptive Gaze

It's possible to penetrate something or someone with just a look. Perhaps you've been on the giving or receiving end of a gaze like that? It's quite powerful, eh?

An active gaze is when you intentionally penetrate with your eyes. A receptive gaze is when you intentionally receive with your eyes.

In this instance, use a receptive gaze.

Allow your eyes to naturally fall on something out in nature that calls to you, or choose something you wish to gaze with.

Instead of observing and thinking, imagine allowing the true nature of whatever you're looking at to penetrate you through your eyes. Feel the energy of it.

Rather than 'doing' this, can you just surrender to it?

Can you surrender and stay present?

Open your heart and be present with curiosity.

If that feels too strange or uncomfortable, then just gently be with this piece of nature as if for the very first time. Notice its colours, shapes and textures. Tune in to it as a living being.

When you're finished, send a little gratitude for the connection.

21. Fire-gazing

This is similar to eye-gazing with nature, but with a single flame or full fire.

Fire-gazing as a meditation is as old as fire itself. Have you ever noticed how people will automatically and naturally gaze at fire? We are drawn to its magical, hypnotic quality.

Fire is life. It brings light and warmth. It helps us stay alive. Our connection to fire is primal and deep. Fire energy can cleanse and burn away that which isn't wanted. It can also serve as a beacon to call in that which you desire.

For fire-gazing meditations, you can light a single tealight or candle or have a full bonfire. You can even visualise a flame!

There are many ways to do fire-gazing meditations, and really, you can't get it wrong. Do what feels right to you at the time.

Here are a few suggestions to get you started:

1. Simple fire-gazing - Gently gaze at a flame or fire for a just a few minutes. As you gaze, soften your focus. Relax your body and deepen your breathing. This alone will help you relax, lower stress and blood pressure, and connect you back to the present moment.
2. Set an intention for clearing and cleansing - As you light your candle or fire, set the intention for it to help burn

off, release or clear energy, thoughts, habits, and patterns that no longer serve you. You can have something specific in mind or just offer a general intention. As you gaze at the flame, imagine it safely burning through your energy system, clearing whatever you've asked to let go of.

3. Set an intention for drawing something to you - As you light your candle or fire, set the intention for the light of the fire to act as a beacon to that which you wish to draw to you. As you gaze at the flame, imagine it sending its light out into the world, out to the very thing/s you want to attract, calling them to where you are.

4. Set an intention for healing - As you light your candle or fire, set the intention for the flame to bring healing energy to you. As you gaze at the flame, imagine the warmth and vibrancy of the fire healing you on every level.

22. Rollercoaster

Believe it or not, it's possible to meditate on a rollercoaster!

My daughter's boyfriend is a mega rollercoaster fan. He has a background in mechanical engineering and has a fascination for how they are put together, how they run, and how they feel to ride as a result of that.

After a recent trip to Alton Towers so that he could ride his favourite, Nemesis, my daughter told me about something she'd witnessed.

She said they'd been riding rides all day and that he wanted to go on Nemesis one more time before they called it a day. She decided to sit it out and let him have the experience to himself. She happened to look up at one point as he went past, and she was struck to see that he had his eyes closed with a blissful, peaceful look on his face.

When he came down, she remarked that he'd been meditating on the ride. After explaining further what she meant — that he was fully present and in the moment with the twists and turns, the movement and gliding through the air — he had to agree. He had indeed been meditating on Nemesis.

His intention had been to really focus on the precision, movement and flow. Yes, it was fun, but that wasn't really why he was riding it at that time. He wasn't looking to engage with another person, figure out what to do next, or see how scary it was. He wanted to tune in to how it felt in that moment.

What a beautiful example of meditation being so much more than just sitting still, trying to clear your mind!

23. Saunatate!

This is one of my favourite ways to meditate! I don't get to do it very often anymore but always make the most of a sauna whenever I can. When I was doing this as a regular practice, here's what I would do:

- Start by setting the intention for anything which no longer serves you to be sweated out of your system with ease.
- Start to take long, slow, deep breaths in and out through your nose.
- Relax your body even more.
- Take your awareness into your centre; breathe and relax.
- Imagine your centre starting to expand in all directions — around you, above you, and below you.
- Allow it to expand for as long as it wants and to grow as big and as vast as it wants for as long as you feel comfortable to do so.
- Stay present with whatever wants to emerge.
- Don't stay in too long. Once you've got a good sweat going or if you feel you're ready, carefully open your eyes and leave.
- Make sure to drinks lots of water during and after, and rest for a bit afterwards.

I often felt like I went on journeys out into the cosmos. Sometimes I just felt super peaceful. Other times, inspiration and ideas flowed freely. Sometimes nothing obvious happened, but I felt changed in a good way. Give it a try and see what happens for you.

24. Floating

You can do this in a bathtub, pool, jacuzzi, ocean or anywhere that you know you are safe to do so. It's pretty simple really.

Lie back and spread your arms and legs out to allow for maximum relaxation, letting go and floating. Allow your breath to deepen and slow down.

Bring your attention to your body. Become aware of where your body meets the water. Notice how they work together, with minimal effort, to keep you afloat.

Imagine that the water is the vast warmth, love and intelligence of the Universe. How would it feel to let go and allow the Universe to hold and support you, just as the water is holding and supporting you now?

How would it feel to just surrender? Relax into deep trust and *know, with your body, heart and soul,* that you are being held and supported all the time.

If you want to, you can set the intention for anything that no longer serves you to flow into the water, where it is instantly transformed.

You can also tune in to the 'enoughness' of the water. There is enough water to keep you afloat, therefore you have 'enough' in your life.

As Mary Poppins says, 'Enough is as good as a feast!'

25. Making art

Making art is one of my favourite ways to meditate. For many years now, I've dabbled in making collages and mixed media art. A long time ago, someone I knew who was an artist told me that collage and mixed media were not real art. So I stopped making it. Crazy, huh?

Then a few years later, I went on my first ever Tantra course. It was a six month 'deep dive' into self-awareness and sexuality. As soon as I got home from the first weekend, I had an incredible deep urge to create, to make art again.

I didn't have any supplies, so I started gathering bits and pieces from around the house, found some glue and probably some cardboard, and went to work.

It was as if I was possessed! Creative energy poured from me. Artwork poured from me. As I worked, I was totally in 'the zone'. Blissed out. In my groove.

Creating art was and continues to be a deep meditation for me. I am utterly present when I am making art. It might take a few minutes for me to 'tune in' and get the creative juices flowing, but once that happens, something magical courses through me. I feel deeply connected to the all-that-is.

This isn't to say that everything I create is magical. Not at all.

What I mean is that I get to experience a magical flow of energy through me. It's a very physical, spiritual experience. As it happens, it was a piece of art I made back then that was partly responsible for my partner and I getting together! That's a story for another time though.

Whether you already know yourself as an artist or not, it's a beautiful way to get present, to *be* present.

This isn't about needing to be good at it or do it in a particular way, and it certainly isn't about doing it for anyone else.

This is another opportunity to be present in your life.

So whether you're painting, sticking and glueing, using crayons, pouring resin, crocheting, carving wood, sketching, sewing, or any other of a million ways you can make art, you can do it as a meditation.

- Be fully present with the desire or urge in you to create.
- Be fully present with whatever it is that wants to come through you, that wants to be given life through your hands.
- Be fully present with the materials and supplies you've chosen to use.
- Be fully present to the colours and textures and shapes.
- Be fully present to how they all mix and match and blend together to make the thing you are creating.

- Be fully present to how your body feels while you are creating.
- Be fully present to your breath while you're creating.

26-27. Shower and bath meditations

There are many delicious and powerful ways to meditate in the bath or shower. Consciously using the element of water can add extra potency to your meditation.

If you don't get a lot of time and space to be alone, are new to meditation or are super busy, then using your bath or shower time as a meditation space is perfect!

Here are a few ideas to get you started:

26. Shower meditations

Sensual - Become aware of the water falling on your skin. Imagine the water caressing you, stroking you as a lover might. Be still and surrender to the flow, the touch. Then move your body in a sensual, erotic way to allow the water to cover the whole of you.

Tune in to your body and ask it which part(s) needs some attention in that moment. Trust your intuition and focus the water there for a moment or two. Use your full senses to engage with the water. Notice the temperature, the pressure, the sound and maybe even the taste of the water.

Clearing I - Stand so that the water is falling right onto the centre of the top of your head. Have the intention for the water to clear and wash away anything that no longer serves you.

Relax your shoulders, jaw and hips. Relax the tiny muscles around your eyes and in your face. Release and let go of any stress, worries or negative energy you are holding in your body. Let it all wash right down the drain. When you feel complete, take a couple of long, slow, deep breaths.

Clearing II - Start with the first clearing exercise. Then move your body so that the water falls on each of your power centres (also known as chakras). After the top of your head (crown), they are:

- **Brow or third eye** - in the middle of your forehead
- **Throat** - at your throat, obviously. With this one, it's good to make sound if you can. Just making a sound on your out-breath is enough. You can also allow any sound that wants to occur naturally. Do whichever feels right at the time.
- **Heart** - centre of your chest
- **Solar plexus** - Place your right hand on your abdomen so that your pinky finger rests just above your belly button. The area under your thumb is the solar plexus area.
- **Sacral** - belly
- **Base** – genitals

Have the intention for the flowing water to clear and wash away anything that no longer serves you at each of these areas. This is an energy clearing and so will happen in, on, and around the body in the area you are focusing on.

Use your intuition to determine how long to stay on each area.

Notice what feelings or thoughts arise as you do this. Just be present with them rather than trying to fix or change them. You may feel a wide range of things from joy to grief, anger to euphoria, sadness to curiosity. Allow them to be there without preference or judgment. Some will clear away, and others will linger. That is perfectly okay.

Healing – There are several ways to experience powerful, healing showers. Give these a try and see what works for you.

- As the water falls over your body, tune in to its healing potential. Your body is 65-70 percent water. Imagine the water activating your body's natural healing processes on a cellular level. Allow the water from the shower to awaken the water molecules in your body. Imagine them feeling refreshed and revitalised. Allow the water to soothe and ease your body, mind and soul.
- Allow the water to envelop you in a warm embrace. Imagine the water holding you, containing you in a safe and loving way. Relax your body and breathe deep. Allow your full self to be nourished, healed and hydrated.
- As you step into the shower, start saying things you're grateful for and see if you can keep going for the whole shower. Start with what is right in front of you:

I'm grateful for

- Hot running water
- Electricity to heat the water
- Shampoo
- Body wash/soap
- Dry towel
- My body – go through each body part if you feel inclined to
- This day

27. Bath meditations

Magical Infusions - When you make a cup of tea, you pour hot water over a tea bag and the contents of the bag infuse into the water to create tea. Similarly, you can infuse your bath water with various things to create something really special, healing and magical.

Once you've chosen what you want to put in your bath, take a moment or two to get grounded and centred. Internally set your intention for this bath. It could be to relax and ease your muscles, to release stress and tension, for spiritual healing, energy cleansing, to heal your body, to connect with the magical or healing properties of the infusion you've chosen, to nurture and nourish yourself, and so on.

Start running your bath, holding your intention and putting whatever you've chosen in the running water.

While you're in the bath, tune in to the oils or salts or whatever. See if you can feel them energetically doing the work you've intended. It's okay if you can't. Tuning in to them gives you an opportunity to be present and to amp up your intentions for the bath.

Immerse yourself in the water and in the energy and qualities of the infusion you've created. Be utterly present with your intention, with the sensations of the water on your body, with your senses.

You could, if you wanted to, say some gratitudes or positive statements while you're bathing. You can also practice some of the breath meditations, but make sure you are safe to do so.

Here are some things you might like to try:

Epsom salts - Good for reducing stress, inflammation and pain. Eases tired muscles, promotes better sleep and use of oxygen in the body. Great for absorbing much-needed magnesium through the skin.

Also good for drawing toxins, both physical and metaphysical, from the body. If your intention is to release 'stuff', then intend for your magically infused bath to help you do so. Feel into the water drawing whatever needs to be released out of you. When you are finished, make sure to rinse off so everything is washed away.

Bubble bath - To remind you to play, have fun and not take life so seriously!

Rose petals or flowers - To soak in and connect to beauty, to feel beautiful, worthy.

Crystals - Use rose quartz to open your heart and connect to love; clear quartz to amplify your intentions, clear energy or gain clarity; amethyst for . . . well, just about everything. You can let the crystals soak in the water and then remove them before you get in or leave them in. Rinse yourself and the crystals when you are finished.

Words and music - Water is well-known to respond to the vibration of words and music. Check out the work of Masaru Emoto for more information about that. You can speak words, qualities, and characteristics you wish to draw to you, pray, or say positive statements directly over or into the water. Play music that has a vibe you'd like to imbue and then soak it in through the water.

Note: Essential oils and herbs are great things to add to a bath but require a bit of health and safety knowledge. Please do your research before adding either of these things to your bath. Never put essential oils directly into your bath without adding to a carrier oil first.

28. Dancing in the rain

There is something magical and very sensual about dancing in the rain. Many years ago, I had a couple of profound dancing-in-the-rain experiences. Both happened at a small, family-friendly festival called Buddhafield.

The first experience happened in the sauna area. There was a lovely couple who brought their mobile sauna to the festival every year.

They had a wonderful set up that included an area for relaxing on carpets and cushions with cups of tea. The husband was often found sitting in the centre of this area, offering full body massages. The sauna itself was in a sort of trailer next to that.

The relaxation area and sauna were both under tarpaulins, so the whole area was rather cosy. There was also a fenced-off outdoor area where you could have a cold shower or cold dip right after your sauna. This area was not covered, but couldn't be seen by the rest of the festival goers.

One particular evening, after spending a rather long time in the sauna and getting deliciously sweaty, I headed out for the cold shower. As I got to the edge of the covered area, there were several other people who had recently left the sauna looking out into the shower area. It was absolutely pouring with rain.

We didn't know each other and had never spoken a word.

Somehow time slowed down; we all looked at each other and just knew we'd shared the same exact thought.

Moving almost as one body, we ran out into the rain, still naked from the sauna. Together we erupted into laughter and dancing and celebration of the magical moment. We got absolutely soaked and loved every minute of it.

There was a profound sense of connection as we looked around at each other, knowing we had shared something really special.

The second experience happened a year or two later at the same festival. I was attending a sort of variety show one evening with some friends. There were about 200 people crammed into a tiny but cosy marquee.

The evening was full of hilarious acts, music and a fantastic MC. He was doing what I can only call spiritual comedy in between the performances.

Towards the end of the evening, he started to talk about how we are all connected and how joy is our natural state and how we are often so stuck in our stories, and wouldn't it feel good to be liberated from them?

The crowd loved him and was pretty hyped up as well as connected through our shared experience of the evening so far. Remember, this was a no-drink, no-drug festival, so this was a natural high we were all feeling.

Eventually, he said something about liberating ourselves by removing a piece of clothing; you know, if we wanted to. This crowd knew his cheeky ways and were all up for it.

Somehow, he weaved his magic and before we knew it, all 200 of us were on our feet, stripping our clothes off and running outside the marquee to dance naked in the rain.

Believe it or not, this was all done in complete silence, as a sort of prayer or meditation. There was a reverence to what we were doing.

Dancing outside, we were invited to connect with ourselves, with each other, with the rain and the stars and moon. It was ecstatic and profound. Easily one of the most profound experiences of my life up to that point.

When was the last time you actively enjoyed the rain? Like *really* enjoyed it? Were fully present with it?

Next time it's raining, take yourself outside and instead of shielding and contracting against it as we often do, open yourself up and allow it in.

Do this wherever you happen to be when it starts to rain, take yourself off to a park or other preferred spot in nature, or just step outside of work or your home if you feel safe to do so.

Spread your arms out wide as if inviting the rain in. Feel the drops on your face and skin without any judgment or preference for things to be different. You can do this in stillness or run around and splash in all the puddles you can find! You can do it naked, half-naked, or fully dressed.

Bring all of your presence to the moment, to the sensations. Dance with the rain! Allow joy to flow and enjoy the moment just as it is.

Note: Use this meditation as a template for reframing other situations or experiences in your life. How can you go from seeing something as a nuisance to seeing it as a joy? How can you go from wishing something away to embracing it as reality?

29-39. Lying on the earth

We humans used to be much more connected to the land, to the earth, than most of us are these days. Long before concrete and roads, we lived and moved in contact with the earth. We walked, slept and worked directly on and with the earth.

We have forgotten that we are part of the ecosystem, not separate from it. Earth has its own frequency, its own electromagnetic energy. Being connected to this energy literally and figuratively keeps us grounded and healthy.

Recent research has shown that lying on the earth and walking barefoot on the earth almost instantly affects our physiology in a positive way. It rebalances our nervous system, can lower stress, reduce pain and inflammation, and even help to improve sleep.

Research has also shown that direct contact with the earth helps to regulate our circadian rhythms (our internal body clock) that regulate digestion, blood pressure, hormones and body temperature for starters.

There's not really any right or wrong ways to lie on the earth. Just lie down and relax! I like to lie with my arms out from my body a bit, either with palms up to the sky or down on the earth — whichever feels right at the time.

Here are a few suggestions for meditating while lying on the earth:

29. Relax your body and allow your breath to deepen

Take a moment to connect to the earth underneath you. Take your awareness down, down, down, and then start to spread it out in all directions around you.

Become aware that you are lying on a small patch of ground that is connected to the rest of the earth.

Become aware of how gigantic the earth is and how you are connected to it right now, in this moment.

Become aware of how you are connected to all living things via the earth.

30. Imagine or allow 'that which no longer serves you' to drain out of you and into the earth

Don't worry, your 'stuff' will be instantly transformed, a bit like manure. You won't cause harm to the earth.

31. Consciously allow your body and energy system to be recalibrated by the electromagnetic energy of the earth

This means to allow the natural energy vibration of the earth to realign you with your own healthy vibration. To calm your nerves, relax your body and generally press the energetic 'reset' button for you. See if you can feel it happening.

32. Imagine growing roots down into the earth

Could be from your feet or from the whole of your body. Follow them down with your imagination as they plant themselves firmly in the earth below you. Tune into them and get a sense of the nutrients from the earth coming up your roots to nourish you.

33. Tune in to the heart and heartbeat of the earth

Even if this doesn't exactly make sense to you, use your imagination and give it a try, see how it feels. As you lay on the ground, take your awareness deep into the centre of the earth.

Imagine you feel or sense a glowing ball of love. Feel it radiating out in all directions and reaching up to where you are. Imagine allowing love from the centre of the earth to penetrate your body and your heart.

Tune in even deeper and see if you sense a heartbeat, a pulse, or other vibration from this deep earth heart. Take some long, slow, deep breaths and relax.

34. Spread your arms and legs out like a starfish and imagine that you can 'float' on the earth

Relax your body and just let go…

35. Once again in the starfish position, deepen your breathing

On each out-breath, relax your body and muscles even more. Now feel how securely and safely the earth is holding you. Allow yourself to feel held, safe and secure.

36. Take your awareness down into the earth

Connect to the earth's consciousness or at least have the intention to. Ask for healing. You can ask for specific or general healing. Tune in and see if you can feel it happening.

37. Tune in to the earth/soil right beneath you

Feel the energy in it. How vibrant and alive it is. Go deeper and deeper, tuning in to the different layers. 'Listen' with your body and awareness. Perhaps you'll get a sense of the history of that piece of land. Maybe the earth will reveal a message for you. Tune in and see what this patch of earth has for you today.

38. Send love into the earth

After relaxing and lying on the earth for an amount of time, drop into your heart. Connect with the Universal, unconditional love that flows to and through your heart. Open your heart a bit wider and send love down into the earth — down and around or as you feel guided to do. Wrap the earth up in a giant ball of loving energy.

39. Plant seeds from your heart

Drop into your heart and reflect on feelings, qualities and experiences you'd like to draw into your life. Imagine each one as a tiny seed that originates in your heart.

Now imagine each seed being planted from your heart into the earth. Visualise or get a sense of this happening. When you've planted all the seeds, send them love, a bit of sunshine and just the right amount of rain. Know in your heart that these things or something even better are on their way to you.

40. Tidying the house

Believe it or not, you can actually make tidying up the house into a meditation. How? By bringing your full presence to it of course.

How often do you complain about having to tidy up? How often do you do it in a bit of a daze, not really present to what you're doing?

What if you were to slow down, be more deliberate, and even practice gratitude as you're doing it?

Here are a few ideas for you:

- Before you begin, drop into your heart. Connect to love so that all of your actions come from a place of love. Remember to breathe deeply.
- As you pick up various items, allow a sense of gratitude to arise. Gratitude for the 'things' that you have, that you've either had the money to purchase or have been gifted. How fabulous that you have these things!
- In Marie Kondo style, if you pick up things that don't bring you joy, recycle them or get rid of them.
- If nothing else, allow the time and energy you spend on tidying to be an act of service to yourself and your loved ones. If you infuse your actions with love, you will feel better as you do it *and* it will infuse your home with love at the same time.

41. Public transport

Travelling somewhere via public transport, whether to work, a fun night out, or a whole other country is a fantastic time to meditate. So often when we're travelling we bring along things to distract ourselves.

We listen to music, read books or newspapers, or anything else to pass the time and avoid having to speak to a stranger. Funny, eh?

Here are a few ways to turn your travel time into being present or meditation time:

A. If you feel safe to do so, close your eyes and take a long, slow, deep breath. Tune in to the rhythm and movement of the transport you are on. Whether bus, train, airplane, ferry or whatever else, it will have a rhythm and cadence. Allow your body to soften a bit. Slow your breath. See if you can become one with the movement, a bit like a surfer with a wave.

B. Relax your body (if it's safe to do so!) and take some deep breaths. Go through your senses one by one and get super present with each one. Close your eyes and listen.

What can you hear? What if you stretch your hearing out a bit further? What are the high-pitched and low-pitched noises?

Then move on to scent and touch.

Eventually, open your eyes. Take in what you are seeing as if seeing it for the very first time. Not just the first time today, but the first time ever. Notice the shapes, colours and textures right in front of you.

C. Just for this moment, gently let go of your fears, assumptions and judgments about others. Drop into your heart and allow it to open to Universal, unconditional love.

Imagine gently sending it out to all the people travelling with you. Don't force it on them as such. Imagine it flowing out in all directions from your heart like a beautiful flowing river.

As it does so, it arrives just outside each person's heart as an invitation. Their energy systems will know it's there and allow it in or not as is right for them.

Don't be attached to who might allow it in or not; just trust the process and allow love to flow.

42. Writing

When I started writing this book back in 2016, I asked the wise people of Facebook how they meditated. One response, in particular, stood out to me. It was about handwriting as a mindfulness practice, which is more or less the same as meditation. Thankfully, the author of the post, Lana Blue, gave me permission to include what they wrote here.

Slow handwriting as a meditation or mindfulness practice

"Often when I write, words flow at light speed, my handwriting becomes almost illegible. Who am I kidding, it IS illegible. Sometimes this is a really helpful technique, and often part of a therapeutic process, just to write and write and write until it stops.

I've recently noticed how my nervous system has been up-regulating during this process – with my body moving into heightened levels of arousal – if I'm comfortable with this heightened state and enjoying the flow of words then that's fantastic.

But I often need to consciously down-regulate, so I can do important things. Like sleep. I use a whole range of techniques to do this.

I recently discovered if I write by hand r e a l l y s l o w l y.

R e a l l y r e a l l y s l o w l y

With a soft lead pencil, relaxing my hand and drawing each individual letter in a mindful way, that my nervous system immediately slows down, and the slower I get the calmer I become.

A wonderful self-discovery – with the added bonus of being able to actually read my own handwriting for a change!"

43. Jo 'Happiness' Howarth's Cup of Tea Meditation

My dear friend Jo 'Happiness' Howarth runs The Happiness Club (**https://www.thehappinessclub.co.uk/**).

It's a fabulous monthly membership club that helps you look after your mental well-being. She is also a speaker, facilitator and author.

When she speaks, she often tells a story of how to be utterly present and grateful while you make a cup of tea. The combination of her beautiful voice, enthusiasm and wonder is a joy to hear.

She has generously allowed me to include her cup of tea journey in this book. Before you read it, take a minute to get still and present. Open your heart. Take a couple of deep breaths. When you are ready, read her journey below as if you've never ever made a cup of tea. Then the next time you make a cuppa, bring your full awareness to what you are doing, just as Jo suggests.

"Let me take you on a journey, a journey to make a cup of tea.

So, you decide you want a cup of tea. You go into your kitchen and open a cupboard. Because you have cupboards on the walls in your kitchen, with doors that open and close to keep the things inside those cupboards safe. You open a cupboard and you take out a mug.

A mug that someone else has made, with their skill and talent and ability, and sold to a shop that you've gone into, with the money that you earned doing whatever it is you do, and decided you like that mug enough to buy it and bring it home and put it in that cupboard, with the door that opens and closes to keep it safe. You take that mug out and you put it on the side.

Then you pick your kettle up and you go over to the sink. You turn the tap and water comes out. Someone has arranged it so that all these pipes come into your house at this exact point so that all you have to do is turn a tap and fresh, clean, amazing, life-giving water comes out of that tap so that you can fill your kettle.

And once your kettle is full, you turn the tap again and the water stops. So your house doesn't flood. Brilliant.

Then you take your kettle over, plug it in, and press a button. Someone else has arranged it so that all these wires come into your house at this exact point so that all you have to do is press a button and it makes that water hot. Not only does it make it hot, it makes it the perfect temperature to make yourself a cup of tea with. Not only does it make it the perfect temperature, it stops itself when it gets there AND it tells you that it's done it.

So that all you have to do is pick that kettle up and pour that boiling hot water onto that teabag in that mug to make yourself a drink that sustains your body and keeps you alive.

Wow.

I find that entire process astounding. Amazing. That we as human beings have the innovation and the intelligence, the ability and the creativity to make something so complicated, so simple. And we pay it no attention whatsoever. We just have a cup of tea.

When you start to look at the world in this way, I promise it will blow your mind."

44 - 47. Meditations using your voice

Your voice is powerful, much more powerful than you may realise. 'Having a voice' can mean different things. It can mean having the ability to speak or to make sounds. It can mean having a say in something, being able to 'voice' your thoughts or opinions, and having a safe space to speak or express your truth.

Many people have grown up hearing the phrase, 'Be seen and not heard' and so have shut down their voices, become afraid or unable to speak up for themselves. Sadly, lots of people have experienced some kind of trauma or been threatened if they were to speak up.

Reclaiming and learning to use your voice, to express your truth, your thoughts and feelings can be very profound. Using your voice in a meditative way is powerfully healing and liberating.

Before beginning any of the voice meditations below, take a moment to get still, grounded and present. Set the intention to use your voice as a meditation and bring your full presence to it.

You could, if you wanted to, take a moment to tune in to your throat chakra first. Bring your awareness to your throat; notice what's going on there, if anything. Pay attention to your throat, neck, jaw, lips, tongue and gums.

Stretch your jaw as if you were trying to pop your ears on an airplane or yawn a couple of times. Stick your tongue out to give it a stretch. Have a sip of water and notice the sensation of it trickling down your throat.

When you are ready, try one of these:

44. Humming

Humming is a way of using your voice without words. Research has shown that humming low notes can relax the nervous system and even reduce stress. My experience of humming low notes is that it is deeply healing and good for getting you present and in your body. Low notes are particularly good for tuning into, healing, and awakening your genitals.

1. Bring your full attention to your throat. Take a deep breath and begin to hum one low note. Notice how it feels. Can you feel the vibration of it in your chest? Your throat? Your genitals? The rest of your body? Hum this low note repeatedly for a while and pay attention to what you feel in your body.

2. Do the meditation above, but this time set an intention for the energy and vibration from your humming to help break up and release stuck energy in your body.

3. Do the original meditation, but this time try using more than one note. Play around with your voice. Notice how it feels to change notes. How does it feel different in your body?

4. Play with humming long, slow notes and then quick, staccato notes. Try humming quietly and then loudly. Hum a song that you love. Keep your awareness on your voice and notice how it feels or what it brings up in you.

45. Singing

Which songs make your soul sing or lift your spirits?

Which song matches your mood in this moment?

What do you wish to express?

Choose a song that resonates with you at this moment or make one up. How does it feel to sing out loud?

Feel how it moves through your body, how it feels to use your voice to express your mood or to change your mood.

46. Speaking

"Be impeccable with your word." don Miguel Ruiz, The Four Agreements

When you are speaking, be mindful of the words you use, your tone of voice, and how fast you are speaking. We spell words and words cast spells.

Practice saying what you mean and meaning what you say. Slow down and be present with your voice and intention as you speak.

Practice speaking meditations by mindfully reading something out loud, either on your own or with someone close to you.

47. Gibberish Meditation

I learned this type of meditation at several neo-tantra workshops. It is believed to have been created by or at least brought to the west by Osho, a controversial modern mystic and teacher.

This meditation is great for releasing an emotional 'charge' around something without going into the story of what happened. Once the charge is released, you can deal with the situation at hand with more clarity, compassion and presence.

This is also good for summoning up and expelling stuck energy, getting things off your chest which you just don't have the words for, getting you out of your head and breaking up negative thinking patterns.

Do this standing or sitting, alone or in a group. If you're worried about someone hearing you, put some music on in the background. Set a timer for fifteen minutes.

Take a moment or two to get grounded and present. Notice your breathing and come into your body.

Start to make gibberish, nonsense, gobbledygook sounds. No actual words are allowed. If you struggle to get started, start with la, la, la, or blah, blah, blah. Allow your voice to come through as it wishes. It might go up or down, make screeching noises, whatever wants to flow out from you. Don't hold back.

Imagine that you're speaking an alien language if that helps, and just keep going. Don't allow sound to stop for the whole fifteen minutes. All sounds are permitted, so you can hum, cry, shout, sing, and so on. Move your body as it wishes to move. Whatever you do, don't allow any silence for fifteen minutes.

When the fifteen minutes of gibberish are up, reset the timer and sit or lie in silence for fifteen minutes. Stay present and relaxed in your body. Follow your breathing.

48-50. Gardening

Working in a garden offers a whole variety of ways to meditate. Whether you're pulling weeds, planting seeds, tilling the earth, spreading fertilizer, or anything else, as long as you're doing it with your full attention and awareness, it becomes a meditation.

Here are some suggestions for you:

48. Preparing a bed or pot

Take a moment or two to connect with the patch of earth or compost you are about to work with. You can tune in to it energetically to make a connection, sit and meditate on it, touch it lovingly with your hands or however you feel naturally drawn to connect.

You can bless the land or send it gratitude and ask it to assist you in growing your plants. When you start to dig or till, imagine working *with* the earth to grow your plants. Bring your full presence to the earth/compost and your purpose for growing these specific plants, flowers or food. Relax your body and breathe.

49. Planting seeds

Once your bed or pot is prepared, you are ready to plant the seeds. Before you put them in the soil, hold them in your hands. Tune into the potential within them. These tiny seeds hold a magical blueprint.

They hold the power and ability to grow into their full potential. Open your heart and send love down your arms, into your hands, and into the seeds. Send them gratitude. Stay fully present as you introduce them to the soil.

50. Watering your houseplants

Fill a container with water. Place your hands on either side of it and bring your full awareness to the water. Open your heart and allow love and gratitude to flow down your arms, through your hands and into the water. As you water your plants, be aware of this love pouring into them, feeding and nourishing them. Connect to each one individually as you water.

51. Falling asleep

There are so many ways to meditate to help you fall asleep that this part could practically be a whole book on its own. Here is one super simple and very effective way for you to try.

Before getting into bed, it's helpful to have some kind of bedtime routine — one that helps you to slow down, relax and unwind.

It's strongly recommended that you switch off your laptop, tablet, phone, and other forms of technology at least one hour before bed. Even better yet, it's recommended that you not have any technology in the bedroom while you're sleeping.

Things that are helpful for getting to sleep:

- Hot/warm bath or shower
- Hot drink
- Sitting still and in silence for a while
- Reading a book
- Classic meditation or other calm, quiet meditations
- Listening to calming music or guided meditations

Here's a lovely meditation for you to try once you're in bed and ready to sleep:

Get comfortable and relax your body. Take some long, slow, deep breaths and really relax your body on the out-breath. Let the bed take the full weight of your body.

Starting at your toes, slowly but surely work your way up your body, bringing your awareness and attention to each body part.

At each part, pause. Take some breaths. Tune in to that particular area and take your breath to it. When you feel in tune or in touch with it, send it a message similar to this: 'Hello, I love you, it's time for sleep now. Relax and go to sleep. Goodnight. I love you'.

Move slowly up your whole body. Focus on each individual area.

Toes (do each one individually if you have the patience or if you go through your whole body and are still awake)

Tops of feet
Bottoms of feet
Ankles
Calves
Shins
Knees (front and back)
Thighs
Hips
Genitals
Lower abdomen
Lower back

Belly
Solar plexus
Spine
Liver
Intestines
Stomach
Gallbladder
Pancreas
Lungs
Heart
Ribs
Chest
Breasts
Shoulders
Upper arms
Elbows
Forearms
Wrists

Backs of hands

Palms

Fingers

Back of neck

Throat

Vocal chords

Jaw

Tongue

Teeth

Gums

Lips

Nose

Cheeks

Eyes

Eyelashes

Eyebrows

Forehead

Brain

Top of head

It's highly unlikely you'll still be awake if you go really slowly, breathe, and focus your attention gently rather than intently. If you find you're still awake, either work your way back down or start over at your toes.

'Hello, I love you, it's time for sleep now. Relax and go to sleep. Goodnight. I love you'.

52. Waiting

What do you usually do when you are waiting? Whether you're waiting for a bus, an appointment or a person to arrive, these days most of us are fiddling with our phones while we wait. We're browsing the internet, playing games, chatting on social media, and even working. Very rarely are we actually just waiting.

To make waiting into a meditation means *not* filling the time and space with distraction.

The next time you have to wait for something or someone, try being present to your surroundings, to the sensations in and on your body.

Be present to the sounds around you. Notice your breath. Tune in to your sense of time. See if you feel time moving.

Notice your thoughts and let them pass on through. Notice how often you want to reach for your phone or some other distraction. Relax and breathe.

53. Using pain

"Pierce some part of your nectar filled form with a pin, and gently enter the piercing and attain to the inner purity." Vijñāna Bhairava Tantra

Part of our human wiring is to run away from pain. It's a good survival technique for sure. Whether physical, emotional, or mental pain, we tend to want to turn away from it, distract ourselves or hide from it.

Here's another way of dealing with or being with pain.

Sit with it. Get fully present to it. Imagine going right into the centre of it. Give it your full awareness and attention.

If you could just be with it without judgement, without preference for it to be different (hard, I know!), what would that be like? Can you breathe into it?

If you're experiencing mental or emotional pain, can you locate it in your body? Ask your body to show you where it is and then focus your soft loving attention there.

For the time being, don't ask it to change or be different. Breathe. Relax. Breathe more.

For a moment or two, can you just be with it?

For a moment or two, can you allow it without pushing it away or wishing it was otherwise?

For a moment or two, can you just bear witness to it?

54-66. Sensory Awareness Meditations

Bringing your full attention to different senses, one at a time, is a profound way of being in the 'now'. Your senses, like your breath, can only ever be in the present moment. So by focusing on them, *you* are in the present moment.

Focusing on sensations allows you to have an embodied experience of presence. That means that you are fully present with what is happening right now, in the moment, rather than your mind's interpretation or evaluation of it.

Learning to experience embodied presence will help you to open up to more joy, more ecstasy and more pleasure.

You can find sweet ecstasy eating a strawberry or smelling your favourite flowers. You can experience deep joy from feeling a breeze on your skin.

These experiences fill you up so that you experience life as rich and bountiful. Then you are not coming into your life and relationships depleted but rather overflowing and abundant, as well as with your senses more finely attuned.

Note: It's often believed that we only have five senses; however, that is very far from the truth. Besides the obvious touch, sound, smell, taste and sight, we also have a sense of the weather, a sense of seasons, temperature, pressure, time, location, direction, and so on.

I read somewhere that we have over sixty senses. For the purposes of these sensory awareness meditations, however, we'll be focusing on touch, sound, smell, taste, and sight.

Here are some suggestions for how to use sensory awareness for meditation:

54. Sensory awareness box

A sensory awareness box is a container of some kind that you fill with different things to calm, soothe or stimulate your senses. You can create a box that is just for one sense, such as touch, or you can create a box that incorporates a few things for each sense.

You can create one that is family friendly or one that is specifically for adult eyes and hands only.

Get a box, basket, crate, backpack, or another kind of container.

Decide if you want it to be specific to one sense or for all of the senses. Think about who is going to use it and what you may or may not want to include. Be mindful of safety and allergies.

Here are some ideas of things to include:

- Things that feel 'nice' such as silky or soft material, shells, rocks, furry things, soft toys or animals, feathers, smooth glass marbles
- Things that are a contrast to 'nice', such as pine cones, rough wool, a scouring pad, rough-edged stones, crunchy leaves, scrub brushes, a toothbrush or a hairbrush
- Wooden toys or spoons
- Stress balls
- Squishy toys/objects
- Cotton balls

- Acorns
- Velvet, silk
- Play-Doh or clay
- Bubble wrap
- Old necklaces or strings of beads
- Paper or material that makes a crinkly sound or feels good to touch
- Different kinds of small bells
- Shakers and rattles
- A musical triangle
- A kalimba (also known as a thumb piano)
- A slide whistle or recorder
- A harmonica
- Party blowers
- Cinnamon sticks
- Essential oils (be careful if you have children using the box)
- Dried coffee grounds
- Scented candle
- Scented pens
- Chocolate
- Mints
- Photos of loved ones, beautiful places in nature or other things that fill your eyes with joy.
- Small pieces of art or swatches of your favourite colours
- Crystals
- Bubbles
- A blanket

- Small cushions
- A mirror
- A small magnifying glass

Add in things like blueberries, strawberries, thinly sliced cucumber or lemon for taste on the day you use the box.

Creating your sensory box can be a meditation in itself as you mindfully choose what you want to include.

Ways to use the sensory box:

Close your eyes or put on a blindfold. Take a moment to get still and present. Take a few deep breaths. When you're ready, reach into the basket and pick up the first thing you're drawn to.

Hold it in your hands and just focus on what it feels like before your mind gets busy deciding what it is. Roll it around in your hands, run it through your fingers, hold it up to your face.

Instead of assuming you know what it is, hold each object as if it were brand new. Explore it with childlike curiosity and a sense of fun.

Once you're sure what it is, engage with it. If it's a musical instrument, explore how to play it. If it's a food item, smell it, lick it, taste it.

When you're ready to experience sight, take off your blindfold and let your gaze rest on whatever is in front of you. Take in the shapes, colours and textures.

Continue for as long as you like.

You can also do this with a partner or child.

One of you is seated comfortably and then blindfolded. The other person slowly and meditatively offers you different things to experience. They might hand you something to feel. They might gently hold an essential oil nearby so that you get a whiff of it. They might play the musical instruments for you or hand them to you for you to explore. Be deliberate in your exploration. Take your time.

Touch

55. Right here, right now

If it's safe to do so, close your eyes right where you are right now. Relax your body. Take a couple of long, slow, deep breaths. Become aware of what is touching you at this moment.

How are your clothes draped on your body? Where are they touching you?

What are you sitting on? Where is your body in contact with what you're sitting or lying on?

Can you feel a breeze or sunshine or rain touching your body in any way? Is the air cool or warm?

What else can you feel right now?

56. Outdoor touch meditation

One of my favourite touch meditations is done outdoors with a partner. You can do this in your garden, in a park, in the woods, or anywhere you feel safe to do it.

One person puts on a blindfold and the other person leads them to a piece of nature and gently places their hands on it.

It could be the trunk of a tree, a flower, a stream, or a patch of grass. The person with the blindfold gently engages, with their full presence, with whatever their hands are placed on.

The person who is not blindfolded takes responsibility for the other person's safety. Make sure they are physically safe and keep your eye on them at all times. Give them plenty of time and space to explore without being rushed. You'll know intuitively when they've had enough, or they can tell you when they're finished with that particular thing.

Lead them to something slightly different for contrast. It's nice to do three or four different things if you can.

It's really lovely to do this in silence if you can. This heightens the sense of touch, bringing a more meditative quality to the experience.

When you're ready, swap over.

Do the whole thing with as few words as possible. This is a meditative space for you both. The 'toucher' focusing on whatever they're touching and the witness keeping you both safe.

Afterwards, you can share your experience of both doing the touching and also holding space for the other.

Note: There are more touch meditations in the Bedroom section.

Sight

57. New eyes

You can do this just about anywhere, but don't do it when you're driving! Close your eyes for a moment and take a couple of deep breaths. Relax your body and bring yourself into your body.

When you're ready, slowly open your eyes and look at your surroundings as if they were brand new. Even if you are doing this at home or somewhere you've been a hundred times, imagine looking through brand new eyes.

What colours do you see? What textures? Where are the shadows? What shapes do you see? What draws your eye to it? Soften your focus and see how that changes things. Look into the spaces in between things. Practice having a neutral, then receptive gaze.

58. Out in nature

Do the same exercise as above, but this time out in nature. You can do it just outside your home, on a beach, in the woods or in your local park. Bear witness to the colours and shapes and textures you see. Take it all in without preference or judgment.

59. Create a space

There are a couple of ways to do this. You can create a special 'sight sensory box' that you use especially for sight meditations. You can put in photos of things, art, people or places that bring you joy or make you feel good. You can put in bits of fabric or anything at all that is a delight for your eyes.

Another way is to create a special place in your home for beauty. It could be a spot on a shelf, counter or dresser, a small table, or anywhere that works for you. Decorate that area with things that light you up, open your heart, and bring joy when you look at them. You can do the gazing meditations here, or just relax, breathe, and enjoy the sights.

Sound

60. New ears

As before, stop right where you are and take in the various sounds in your environment. Close your eyes if it's safe to do so. Relax your body, take a few deep breaths, and just listen without judgement or preference.

Imagine you've never heard these sounds before. Rather than indulging your curiosity and trying to figure out what they are, quieten your mind and just allow the sounds to float to and through you. Allow them to be pure sensation.

What do you notice or feel? What tones, textures, depth, pace and patterns might you be aware of? How many different sounds can you hear? What do the sounds *feel* like?

61. Select sounds

Consciously choose sounds that either fit the mood you're in or help access a mood or feeling you want to experience. For example, you can play a piece of music you like, phone someone whose voice you'd like to hear, play an instrument, tap on your body, or use your voice.

62. Sound box

Create a sensory box just for sound. Include a variety of sound-making things. These could be little bells, chimes, shakers, and other instruments. You could also include things like crunchy leaves, paper to rustle or wooden spoons to tap on things around you.

Smell

Smell is one of our most powerful, primal senses. It is considered to be the first sense we develop, and due to how it is processed in the limbic area of the brain, it's known to trigger memory and emotion.

One Christmas, while we were opening presents with the family, my partner's twin brother opened a gift that contained a bottle of shower gel. He opened it up, as you do, and smelled it. "Oh, wow!", he exclaimed. He handed it to my partner and asked him what the smell reminded him of. Instantly, my partner said, "The basement in Germany."

When they were about fifteen years old, they lived on an army base in Germany. My partner said if you'd have asked him what the basement there smelled like, he would have had no idea. He wouldn't have thought of it as having a smell. Yet as soon as he and his twin brother smelled some random shower gel, a memory was evoked.

63. This moment

Pause for a moment, wherever you are, and just notice the scents around you. Try to do this without judgement or preference. Take some long, slow, deep breaths in and see what you can detect. Are the smells around you familiar? Nice? Not nice? Do they trigger emotion or memory in you? Can you just be with whatever arises in you?

64. You choose

What are your favourite smells? Some typical things that people like to smell include:

- Roses or other flowers
- Cinnamon
- Vanilla
- Bread baking
- Fresh cut grass
- Chocolate
- Coffee
- Old books
- Your lover
- A campfire

Instead of just carrying on when one of these gorgeous scents is in your vicinity, stop and take the opportunity to be present with it. Or make a special effort to have things nearby that you like to smell.

Relax your body. Relax your jaw and the muscles of your face. Relax your shoulders.

Get present in your body.

Take a long, slow, deep breath.

Notice your reaction to the smell. Be utterly present with it.

Taste

65. Right here, right now

Close your eyes and bring your attention to your mouth, lips and tongue just as they are right in this moment. Is there a particular taste in your mouth? Move your tongue around slowly and search for any taste that might be there. Maybe there's a whisper of the last thing you ate? Or the toothpaste you used earlier? Maybe you can taste the lip balm you applied? Maybe there's no particular taste at this time. Lick your lips and feel into your mouth to see what tastes might be there.

66. Taste ritual

Select three or four things you like (or don't like!) and one by one, slowly but surely, put one on your tongue and bring your full awareness to it. This is lovely to do blindfolded as it heightens your other senses. Do it slowly, as a meditation.

Choose things not only for taste but for texture too. Although this is primarily a taste meditation, our mouth and lips are very sensitive to touch. Taking time to tune into the textures as well as the taste can be very erotic!

When I offer sensory awakening rituals to clients, I often use these for taste:

- Blueberries
- Papaya or melon
- Strawberries (take a moment to take in their aroma before tasting)
- Different kinds of chocolate (see chocolate meditation below)
- Fizzy water (more for texture than taste)
- Salt granules
- Thinly sliced cucumber
- Thinly sliced lemon

Note: If you are doing this for a friend, lover or client, make sure you ask about allergies or food intolerances in advance.

67-68. Meditative meals

67. In the kitchen

The next time you're about to prepare a meal, or even a snack, take a moment before you begin to get present, to open your heart and take a few deep breaths.

Come fully into your body and the present moment.

As you begin to chop, slice, and stir, tune in to the ingredients you're cooking. Allow a feeling of gratitude for the food and for the people that grew the food for you, for the soil that the food was grown in, for the journey that the food took to get to your city, the shop you went in to get it, and to yourself for getting it.

Thank the food for offering up its nutrition and vibration for your well-being. Prepare your food with love and gratitude.

68. At the table

Now that you've taken the time to prepare your food as a meditation, why not enjoy eating it that way too? So often we sit in front of the telly or computer while eating instead of being present with what we're doing.

Take a moment to settle into eating mode rather than cooking mode. Take another moment to look at your food, the colours and textures. Notice the plate or bowl it's in.

Slowly put a bite in your mouth and bring your full awareness to it. Notice the temperature, taste and texture. Can you feel the love you imbued it with while you were cooking? Can you tune in to the nutrition or vibration of the food? Eat each bite mindfully and not only will you enjoy it more, but it will also aid your digestion!

69. Chocolate meditation

One of my absolute faves! You can actually do this with any food item, but chocolate lends itself particularly well.

There are probably a million ways to do a chocolate meditation. I'm going to keep it super simple for you and just offer two here. I would love to hear your favourite ways to meditate with chocolate.

Informal - Rather than just munching your way mindlessly through a piece of chocolate or chocolate bar, barely even registering what you're doing, take time to eat it slowly and deliberately. Take a moment to savour it. Smell it. Take a small bite and just let it sit on your tongue for a moment. Feel it start to melt. Take a deep breath and continue to enjoy your chocolate with your full presence.

Formal - Do this as a sort of ritual. Choose one or several special, favourite kinds of chocolate. Lay them out deliberately on a plate you like, maybe one reserved for 'fancy' dinners. Take some time to get really present. Maybe start with a few minutes of Classic Meditation.

When you are ready, gaze at the chocolates. Take in their colour, size and texture. Allow and enjoy the feeling of anticipation as it arises. Don't rush. Choose one to start with and pick it up. Inhale its scent deeply, as you might inhale the delicious, familiar scent of your lover. Does it make your mouth water?

Place it against your lips and just feel it. Eventually, lick it, or nibble it, or place it on your tongue. Hold it gently in your mouth as you start to become aware of its flavour. Allow it to begin to melt without chewing it. Delight in the texture and taste of the melting chocolate.

Allow it to fully melt if you have the patience, or go ahead and chew it, but do so slowly and deliberately. Take your time and be fully present with each piece. When you are finished, stay in your meditative state for a while. Don't rush back into 'doing' mode.

Chapter 8
Meditations for Business Success

"Meditation, more than anything in my life, was the biggest ingredient of whatever success I've had." Ray Dalio, the billionaire founder of Bridgewater Associates, the world's largest hedge fund firm

"It's almost like a reboot for your brain and your soul . . . it makes me so much calmer when I'm responding to emails later." Padmasree Warrior, CTO, Cisco Systems

"The journey of true success and lasting leadership begins with the inward journey to the soul." James Arthur Ray

As mentioned earlier in the book, what 'success' looks like in business terms is changing, thankfully! Power and money are no longer the only markers of success. These days, people want to know about a business's carbon footprint, what causes they support, and how they treat their employees.

Mindfulness, resilience training, and even yoga and breath workshops are being taught in businesses, from the big corporates to the smaller start-ups. Why?

Because it's finally being recognised that taking care of your team, your staff, is good for business. A person's well-being will directly impact how they perform, how they feel about coming to work, how often they call in sick and how they talk about your business.

Building good, long-term practices for mental, emotional, physical, and even spiritual health makes total sense when you look at the bigger picture of business success. Whether you are running your own business or working in someone else's, you and your colleagues will benefit from regular meditation.

The meditations below are specifically designed to be used while you're at work. They can be used in a variety of work settings. Adapt them as you need to so that they work for you.

70. Three deep breaths

Take three long, slow, deep breaths in through your nose. Really fill up your lungs. Breathe out of your mouth, making a little sound, just like a deep sigh. Relax your body deeply on the out-breath. If you feel drawn to do so, you can intend to 'release anything which no longer serves you' on the out-breath.

71. Focused breathing

You can do this for as long as feels right or set a timer for one to five minutes. Breathe as outlined above — long, slow, and deep. Pay attention to your breath as it enters your nose and travels down to your lungs.

Be aware of the rise and fall of your chest. Relax more deeply on each out-breath. Use your imagination to direct your out-breath to any specific tension or contraction in your body to help it release and let go.

Allow stress to drain down your body and out through the soles of your feet. Breathe this way until you intuitively feel complete or until your timer goes off.

72. Notice your body

Close your eyes, relax, take a couple of deep breaths. Become aware of the outline of your body. Using your awareness, or mind's eye, follow it from your head, down one side, around, and back up the other side. Become aware of what your shoulders are doing. Roll them back and forth a few times. Allow them to relax. Notice how you're feeling.

73. Drinking water

A quick, simple, and easy way to meditate at work is to do it while you're drinking water. Not only will you get the benefits of meditating, but you'll also get the benefits of staying hydrated.

Grab a cup or bottle of water. Sit with your feet flat on the ground, back straight, shoulders relaxed. Take a couple of long, slow, deep breaths and allow your body, shoulders and jaw to relax even more.

Have the intention to be fully present while you drink some water. Bring your cup or bottle slowly to your mouth. Be aware of the feel of it pressing against your lips. Slowly allow some of the water into your mouth. Hold it there for just a moment. Imagine that you can feel its life-giving properties. Imagine that you can feel how good it is for you.

Allow gratitude to bubble up as you swallow the water. Pay attention to it as it flows into your body. Imagine it loving you from the inside, hydrating your cells and organs.

When you're ready, take another sip. Pay attention to how it feels on your tongue, in your mouth before you swallow it. When you've finished, take another couple of long, slow, deep breaths.

Note: It's important that this meditation is done with water rather than tea or soda or any other drink. That's because other drinks are usually either dehydrating, full of chemicals, or in some other way not very good for you. Water is necessary for life, for good health, on every level. Sip it throughout your day. Sip it with presence — even better!

74. Mindful lunch

If at all possible, take time and space for a mindful lunch. What, I hear you ask, is a mindful lunch? Well, a mindful lunch can be several different things. The core of which is presence, of course.

A mindful lunch could be:

- Finding a place to sit and eat outside in nature.
- Tuning in to your environment while you are eating.
- Eating slowly and deliberately.
- Tuning in to the tastes and textures of the food you're eating.
- Tuning in to how your body receives the food you're eating.
- Taking some time to do one or more of the other meditations in this book during your lunch break.

75. Quick grounding technique

Life and work can be quite hectic at times. Our attention is drawn in different directions and it's quite normal to get a bit dizzy or distracted with it all. This is a quick grounding technique that will bring you back down to earth, back into your body and into the present moment.

Once you're grounded and back in your body, clarity, and most certainly presence, tends to follow. You can do this for one to two minutes or as long as you feel the need to.

You can do this sitting or standing, on your own at your desk, or even subtly in a meeting if you need to!

Place your feet flat on the floor. If you can be barefoot or at least take off your shoes, that is a bonus. It will work whether you have your shoes on or off.

So, feet flat on the floor. If you can, close your eyes. Relax your body. Roll your shoulders forward and backwards a couple of times. Allow your breath to get deeper and slower.

Become aware of your feet on the ground. Take your awareness, or your mind's eye, deep down into the earth. Imagine travelling down past all the various layers of earthy goodness.

Go down as far as feels comfortable to you at that time. You might find yourself right in the fiery centre! Fantastic!

Taking long, slow, deep breaths, imagine your in-breath drawing that rich, grounding, nutritious energy up into your body through the soles of your feet.

Once you feel it flowing, invite it to travel all the way up both legs to your hips and genitals. Take a few more breaths and really fill up your whole pelvic area.

Then continue using your imagination and breath to draw the nourishing earth energy up the centre of your body, into your heart. This is your heart centre, in the middle of your chest. Really fill your heart to overflowing with earth energy.

If you feel present and grounded, you can stop here.

If you want to keep going, draw more earth energy up into your shoulders, your neck and throat, your jaw, face, brain, and all the way up to the top of your head.

Take as much as you need. The earth is rich and abundant, so you can really fill your boots.

When you are finished, take your awareness back to the soles of your feet. Press them into the floor to really plant yourself firmly back in the present moment.

76. Walking meditation

Meditations 15-18 in the Life section are all walking meditations. If you can get outside the office and into some nature for these, that would be wonderful! However, you don't even have to leave the office to benefit from a walking meditation.

As you move through the office, become conscious of your steps. Pay attention to how your foot lands heel first and then gently rolls towards the ball and toes.

Take slow steps. Be deliberate. Just walking to another person's desk or office can become a meditation if you bring your presence to it.

77. Simple positive statements

Sometimes you need something quick and powerful to bring you back into the present moment, to get you focused and ready for whatever is next. Simple, positive statements call your brain and body to attention. Find one that works for you and repeat it to yourself at least three times. You can say them silently in your mind, or better yet, say them out loud.

You can make up your own or try these:

- I am present, I am ready.
- I've got this.
- Relax, relax, relax.
- I can do it.
- I am confident.
- I am relaxed and focused.

78. Pre-paving

Pre-paving is a way of using presence, intention and visualisation to create a path to something you'd like to create or see go well. It could be an interview, a meeting or presentation, or an important phone call.

This isn't dissimilar to athletes who visualise themselves winning the match or crossing the finish line. It's been scientifically proven that your brain doesn't know the difference between really crossing the finish line or just imagining it.

So the more you visualise it while also creating the feeling of what that would be like, the more you are wiring your brain and energy system to actually create the thing you want.

There are a few ways to do this. The most important thing is to find a way that works well for you.

Remember, you might be a visual person who actually 'sees' things in your mind's eye, or you might just get a sense or feel of it. Either is fine and will still work.

As you summon up the thing you want to pre-pave, imagine the best possible outcome. What would that look like? What would you be seeing if that was happening? Who would be there with you? How would you be feeling emotionally? How would your body feel? Allow those feelings to arise in your body.

You don't have to see or know every single detail, the *feeling* of what's happening is more important. Here's an example for you:

Dream job interview

You have applied for your dream job and have been called in for an interview.

Find a comfortable place to sit or lie down. Relax your body. Take some long, slow, deep breaths. Relax your body even more.

When you feel relaxed, imagine the feeling of waking up the morning of the interview full of confidence and excitement. Watch yourself as if watching a film. You throw back the covers feeling rested and rejuvenated after a great night's sleep.

You go about your morning with a smile on your face and a little skip in your step. Notice how that feels in your body right now.

You already know what you're going to wear because you planned ahead and prepared it last night. Slipping into that outfit expands your confidence and makes you feel and look great! Have a look at yourself in the mirror and give yourself a cheeky smile.

You have a healthy breakfast that energises you and your body, and you leave for the interview. Your journey there is super smooth and easy and you're walking on air as you arrive.

You are warmly welcomed at the new company and have a lovely chat with the person who greets you. You feel relaxed, comfortable and confident.

The interviewer arrives, and you hit it off immediately. Conversation flows, and you answer all the questions with ease. Notice how relaxed and calm your body is.

As you leave the interview, you just know that the job is yours if you want it. Notice how it feels in your body to know that.

79. Building confidence

Confidence is a bit of a slippery character. You can feel confident on some days and not on others. You might feel confident in your ability to do some of your work, but not other parts. That is perfectly normal.

The good news is that you can actually build and cultivate confidence.

Here is a simple, powerful confidence-building meditation for you:

Make like Superman

Eastern mystics and ancient practices have long known that you can use your body to shift your physiology and therefore your mind, thoughts, feelings and behaviours. Harvard researcher Amy Cuddy has actually done the scientific legwork to prove how it works. For more detailed information, check out her TED talk on body language and her book called *Presence*.

The gist of it, in terms of building confidence, is this: When you contract your body, become physically smaller, and breathe shallowly, your body thinks you are in danger or are scared. So it prepares you for fight, flight or freeze. You produce more cortisol and testosterone. This keeps you alert but also stressed, ready to run. You will feel scared and less powerful rather than confident.

When you expand your body, stretch out, take up space, breathe more deeply and stand up tall, your body raises testosterone and lowers cortisol. This means you are alert and present and also relaxed. Perfect for feeling confident and grounded.

So the next time you need a boost of confidence, make like Superman. Here's how:

- Take a minute to stand up and move around. Stretch your arms wide and yawn.
- Shake out your legs and wiggle your hips.
- Now assume the superman pose! You know the one — spine straight, chest up, head up, hands on hips, confident as hell!
- Hold the pose for a minimum of two minutes.
- Keep your body and breath relaxed.
- Your body will be busy raising testosterone and lowering adrenaline and cortisol.
- This gives you the perfect blend of confidence chemicals!
- When your two minutes are up, take a couple of deep breaths and see how you feel.

80. Access Your Inner Business Guru

Ok, I know the word 'guru' gets thrown around a lot these days, and perhaps it has lost all meaning. So what the hell is an 'inner business guru' and why might you want to access yours?

Your inner business guru is the part of you that just 'knows'.

- It knows how to help you make good business choices and decisions.
- It knows what your business needs to flourish.
- It knows who you need to call, e-mail, or contact.
- It is the inner knowing, the inspired voice from within.
- It is the leader inside you, guiding you.
- It knows how to help you grow your business.

Every one of us has the capacity to tap into 'Infinite Intelligence'. Infinite Intelligence is the collective consciousness, the creative flow of the Universe, the wisdom of Source energy.

'I know this world is ruled by Infinite Intelligence. It required Infinite Intelligence to create it and it requires Infinite Intelligence to keep it on its course … It is mathematical in its precision'. Thomas A. Edison

Your inner business guru is a particular strand of infinite, Universal intelligence that you can access for guidance and help.

Your inner business guru is 100 percent in alignment with what you and your business need to grow and expand, to evolve, and to serve its highest purpose.

'We must stop planning, plotting and scheming, and let Infinite Intelligence solve the problem in its own way'. Florence Scovel Shinn

If you've had any success in business, you've probably already been listening to your inner business guru. It has endless ways of communicating with you.

- The idea that wakes you up in the middle of the night.
- The lyrics to the song you heard at the gym that inspire a solution to a problem.
- Running into an old colleague at lunch and realising it's time to collaborate.

In order to really hear the whispers, the inspiration, the hunches, you have to get out of the way . . . and really, out of your mind.

This is why a lot of people get inspiration in the shower or when they're on holiday.

Their mind isn't trying to tackle a problem to the ground whilst doing a million other things at the same time.

It's enjoying the hot water or lying in the sunshine.

When your thinking mind is out of the way, the inner wisdom can be heard.

How to access your Inner Business Guru:

- Find somewhere comfortable to sit or lie down. Close your eyes and relax your body.
- Take some long, slow, deep breaths. Allow your body to relax even more.
- Imagine yourself sitting somewhere beautiful, somewhere you feel safe.
- Notice that next to you is an extra chair, and you notice someone walking towards you.
- As the person approaches, you recognise them. They are your inner business guru (IBG).
- Note: Not everyone visualises in the same way. You might just get a sense of them rather than seeing them in full Technicolor. That is totally okay.
- Invite your IBG to sit down with you.
- Tell them about the situation you have going on or a problem you'd like some help with.
- Trust that they absolutely have your best interests at heart and that they want to help.
- Listen to what they have to say and discuss anything else you want to at this time.
- When you are finished, remember to thank them before they get up and leave.
- Take a minute to allow their wisdom and guidance to sink in or integrate.

81. Put it in the toaster - a meditative way to solve problems

This was my mum's wisdom for trying to solve a problem: put it in the toaster and see what pops up.

She knew that if you could get out of the thinking mind for a while, you'd be more likely to access the inspiration or wisdom or solution you were looking for.

It's a bit like when amazing ideas come to you when you're driving or cooking — doing anything other than concentrating on the problem at hand.

Here's how to 'put it in the toaster':

- Take a minute to focus inwards.
- Tell your body, heart, and mind that you need an answer, idea or solution. Explain the situation, briefly.
- If you want, you can let your system know that you need the answer by the end of the day, or in two hours, or whenever.
- Get on with your day and trust that the answer is on its way to you.
- Pay attention to thoughts, ideas and signs that pop up over the next few hours or days.

82. Quickfire gratitude round

Stop whatever you're doing. Take a long, slow, deep breath in and out. Relax your body.

Think of three things you're grateful for.

You can just think them quietly to yourself, say them out loud, or write them down. Why not write them on a Post-it Note and put it where you can see it for the rest of the day?

Chapter 9
Meditations for Bedroom Success

When I first started working in the realms of sexuality, conscious sexuality and neo-tantra, the question I got asked the most was, 'Can you teach me methods and techniques for being a better lover'.

My answer was always the same.

Yes, I can. However, no method or technique in the world will work if you are not present. If you are not showing up fully. If you are not allowing yourself to be vulnerable. If you are not being a safe space. If you don't have good communication skills or understanding and respect for boundaries and consent.

With these meditations for bedroom success, I want to invite you to do some self-reflecting, to deepen your knowledge and experience of who-you-really-are. That's the real foundation of being an amazing lover. Owning and loving all of who you are.

Being willing to bring this full self to your connections, to intimacy, and to the bedroom.

Your sexuality and how you express it should never be dependent on another person. Meaning, whether you're in a relationship or not, it's up to you to maintain your connection to your sexual self. It's up to you to keep your own flame burning, to find ways to express all of who you are, including your sexual self.

Becoming a better lover with someone else requires it.

Meditations with Self

83. Being with your sexual energy

Quite often, when we feel our sexual energy, when we feel aroused, we think we have to do something with it. We think we need to either masturbate or be sexual with someone else as if that's all that energy is for.

We look for ways to extinguish the energy rather than luxuriating in it. I'm not saying that orgasms are bad, not at all! I've just so often heard people say they don't know what to do with all that energy and so they feel like they have to release it.

There are huge health and pleasure benefits to just being with that energy, to learning a variety of ways to engage with it and express it.

Find a comfortable place to sit or lie down. Relax your body, shoulders, face and jaw. Take some long, slow, deep breaths and relax your body even more.

Think your sexual energy on.

There are several ways to do this.

- You can just 'think' it on. Try it and see what happens. This might feel like noticing that it's on, deciding it's on, or encouraging or allowing it to be on.

- Take your awareness or mind's eye to your genitals, hips, and thighs and think or say the intention for your sexual energy to 'switch on'.
- Use your in-breath to draw sexual energy in from the Universe. Draw in as much as you like on your long, slow, deep in-breath and release it into the whole genital/hip/thigh/belly/lower back area on your out-breath.
- Imagine lighting a pilot light in your base chakra (genital/hips/thighs/ass area).
- Use a bit of humour and your favourite superhero command! "Go, go sexual energy power!" "Sexual energy is GO!" "By the power of sexual energy!"
- Issue a gentle invitation. If your sexual energy is particularly quiet or has been tucked away for safety, don't rush it or yourself. Tune into your body with love and patience. Imagine issuing a loving invitation from your heart, from your body, for your sexual energy to emerge as and when it's ready.

If thinking it on doesn't work for you, that's okay. Keep trying. In the meantime, try the options below, either on their own or with the 'think' suggestions above:

- Squeeze your PC muscles — the ones you use to stop a stream of urine.
- Gently move your hips. Make small circles that eventually widen out and back in again or try a gentle thrusting motion.

- Use your hands, but only very gently and softly, to awaken the energy. Then remove your hands.

Most of the time you will feel a warmth, tingle or buzzing sensation in your genitals and/or in surrounding areas. If you experience your sexual energy in other parts of your body, think it on there.

This may or may not feel like arousal. You may or may not be 'ready for sex'. That's not really what we're aiming for here.

We're just allowing that potent sexual energy to be 'on'. To see how it feels when we witness it and sit with it, rather than demanding or expecting something of it or getting rid of it.

Now that it's on, just be with it. Become aware of it. Notice how it feels. It might be super quiet and gentle or loud and roaring. However it feels is perfect.

Slow your breathing a little and continue to stay present. Can you feel it in one part of your body or more? Where is it? What thoughts or feelings arise? Breathe and just be.

84. Magic dial

Start by doing the meditation above (Being with Your Sexual Energy). Once you are aware of your arousal or sexual energy, imagine that you have a magic dial. You might visualise it or just have an intuitive sense of it.

This magic dial controls the amount of sexual energy you can feel. Turning it up cranks up the amount of sexual energy flowing through you. Turning it down quietens that energy.

Please note: Turning this dial all the way up does not mean that you are suddenly erect or wet and ready for penetration. This isn't about 'getting ready for sex'. It just means that the channel through which sexual energy flows in you is wide open. You may or may not experience 'readiness' for sex.

Using your intention and imagination, experiment with turning this dial up and down.

Do it slowly and deliberately.

How does it feel if you turn it down way low, to where the energy is only just detectable?

How does it feel if you turn it up and up and up?

Where is your comfortable edge in this moment? Although sexual energy is infinite, you will most likely find an edge that is right for you at this time. Your comfortable edges will change just as your mood, desires and tastes change and evolve. Be present with how your energy feels in the now.

When you've finished experimenting, find a comfortable setting and leave the dial there. It will return to autopilot when you are not directly focusing on it.

85. Adding breath to the magic dial

If you didn't quite get on with the magic dial, or if you'd like to advance your explorations of it, you can add in some conscious breathing.

Once again, start with the 'Being with Your Sexual Energy' meditation. Summon up your magic dial.

Begin to take long, slow, deep breaths in and out through your nose. Now imagine using your in-breath to turn up the dial, to expand your sexual energy channel. Allow more sexual energy to flow or arise on the in-breath, and let it settle and expand into your body, at that expanded place, on the out-breath.

Use your breath to draw that energy up the centre of your body. Start by drawing it up into your heart centre, in the middle of your chest. This time use your in-breath to draw the energy up and your out-breath to release it into your heart, so that your heart becomes full of sexual energy.

Feel, sense, or imagine that raw, powerful sexual energy blending with the Universal, unconditional love in your heart. Feel what happens when they connect.

Do this in small increments, following the flow of energy as you do so. If your body or energy system is telling you to do something a little differently, trust your intuition and give it a try.

86. Breathing sexual energy around your body

Now that you've experienced using your breath to crank up your magic dial, you're ready to use your breath to move sexual energy around your body.

Why would you want to do that?

- It feels amazing.
- It's nourishing and nurturing for your body and soul.
- It is good for your health.
- It expands your creative and erotic potential.
- It creates new ways to experience your sexual energy.
- It helps you to feel and be present in your body.
- It expands your capacity for full body orgasms.
- It deepens and expands your capacity for pleasure.

Start with the 'Being with Your Sexual Energy' meditation. Eventually, start to take long, slow, deep breaths. Keep relaxing your body, your jaw and your breath.

After a few moments, use your in-breaths to move sexual energy up through your body. Imagine that as you breathe in, slowly and deeply, your sexual energy rises up through the inside of your body.

Use your in-breath to draw sexual energy upwards the way you would suck a drink through a straw. Pull up on the in-breath, and on the out-breath, imagine releasing that energy into your body, your organs, your skin, and bones.

Breathe your sexual energy up to meet your heart. Really fill your heart with it.

Imagine it moving into your lungs, your liver, your kidneys. Use your breath, intention and imagination to breathe your sexual energy into your bones, your cells, your DNA.

Feel it energising, healing and enlivening all the various parts of you. Sexual energy is like the fountain of youth, so allow that nectar to really fill you up. Allow it to seep deep into your bones, your bloodstream, and your very molecules.

You might feel it as tingling or warmth or buzzing or something else. You might not even feel it every time. Trust that it's working and practice it regularly.

87. Connecting sexual energy and heart energy

The two biggest energies we have access to are our sexual energy and love. Not conditional, egoic love, but Universal, unconditional love. On a metaphysical level, this is what you are. You are Universal, unconditional love.

Sexual energy on its own is delicious, nutritious and deeply nourishing. However, it is also a raw, wild, primal energy that is refined by moving through or being connected to the heart.

Why would you want to refine this energy?

Think of sexual energy like electricity for a moment. If a wire that has electricity moving through it is connected to a lamp or a toaster, that electricity is useful and helpful. If the wire is just flapping about in the wind with electricity pouring out, it is dangerous and can cause harm.

Wild, raw sexual energy is powerful stuff. Sure, you can have sex with it, but more often than not, that type of sex is not the sex you're looking for. It's not connected, grounded or conscious. It's usually an empty experience and not nearly as nourishing and fulfilling as it could be.

Start with the 'Being with Your Sexual Energy' meditation. Once you feel your sexual energy buzzing away, start to use your breath to draw it up into your heart. Use your in-breath to draw it up and on the out-breath, imagine releasing all that gorgeous sexual energy into the centre of your heart.

This is not just your actual, physical heart. This is your 'heart centre' or 'heart chakra' located in the centre of your chest. Physically, it includes your heart, lungs, thymus gland and ribs. Metaphysically, it includes love, compassion and empathy — for self and others.

Imagine that as you release sexual energy into your heart centre, your heart expands in all directions. Become aware of the Universal, unconditional love in your heart.

Imagine or become aware of these two energies merging in your heart. Really fill your heart with this blended energy. Take time to notice how it feels different to sexual energy on its own. Feel how powerful it is.

You can use your breath to spread it around your body, or just sit with it, be with it.

88. Spreading sexual-heart energy around your body

Start with the 'Connecting Sexual Energy and Heart Energy' meditation. When your heart is full of sexual energy and you feel a steady flow, start to use your in-breath to move the energy from your heart to other parts of your body.

As in previous meditations, use your breath, intention, and imagination.

Tap into the overflowing, infinite cauldron of sexual-heart energy in your heart centre and deliberately move and release it into your organs, your cells and your DNA.

Notice how this energy feels different to raw sexual energy. Notice how it feels fuller, less jagged, more enriching, more powerful.

Breathe it up your spine.

Breathe it into each chakra — for clearing, for energising, for healing, for opening, for recharging, and so on.

89. Breast meditation

Whatever your gender, your breasts may or may not feel like a part of your sexual anatomy. Some people experience little to no sensation in their breasts or nipples, while others find them deeply erotic, sensual, and sexual areas of their bodies.

Whatever is true for you is perfect. You are perfect as you are.

It's also very possible that your experience of your breasts will change over the course of your lifetime. They may be more sensitive for a while, and then not sensitive at all. They may go from being fairly unresponsive to becoming your most pleasurable body part and back again.

However you're experiencing them in this moment, it's very powerful to connect with them and create a new relationship with them.

This breast meditation is for everyone, regardless of gender or sexual preference.

Even if you have had a mastectomy or similar operation, you still have 'energy breasts', the energy of where your breast would be if it were physically there. You can still do this meditation, and in fact, although possibly challenging at first, it can be a great doorway into deeper healing.

It's an opportunity to 'meet and greet' your breasts in a safe way, with openness and curiosity.

You can do this with your clothes on or off, your breasts covered or not.

There will be an opportunity to touch your breasts, and you may do so however you feel most comfortable. Directly on your skin or over clothing, a sheet or towel. You can do it without touch at all. You can do this on your own or with a partner.

I'd recommend doing this with your eyes closed at first as that allows you to go more deeply into your body and the experience. Ultimately there is no right or wrong way to do this — do what feels safe and right for you.

Find a comfortable place to sit or lie down.

Close your eyes and allow your body and mind to settle. Start to take long, slow, deep breaths in and out through your nose. Allow your body to relax even deeper. Relax the muscles of your face and your jaw. Relax your shoulders and your spine. Relax your hips and let the floor, bed, or whatever you're sitting on take the full weight of your body.

Continue with the long, slow, deep breaths.

Bring your awareness to your heart centre, right in the centre of your chest. Take a minute to connect to your heart, the seat of love and compassion.

Notice that your breasts are located in the same region as your heart, like an outward pouring of your heart. Start to become more aware of your breasts.

Super Simple Version

Gently place your hands on your breasts and bring your full presence, your full awareness to them. Notice if any thoughts or feelings arise, and just let them go. Stay present with them for as long as you wish. When you are finished, send them some love. Take a long, slow, deep breath in, and as you breathe out, you can remove your hands from your breasts.

Longer Version

At first, without touching them, see if you can use your awareness, your mind's eye or intuition, to travel to and around the shape of each of your breasts. Take your time.

Can you sense the size and shape of your breasts?

Notice the weight of them.

Become aware of your nipples. What feelings stir in you when you allow yourself to become aware of your breasts and nipples?

See if you can trace the outline of your breasts with your mind, your awareness. Follow the curves out from your chest, around and up and over one breast and then the other.

Allow yourself to become aware of the tissue of your breasts, the inner connective tissues, and the outer fleshy tissue.

If you feel moved to, place your hands gently on or over your breasts. How do they feel? How do they receive your touch? How do they feel in your hands? Can you be with them just as they are, without judgement or preference, and just accept them as they are?

Take some long, slow, deep breaths. Relax your body even more.

Tuning in more deeply to your breasts, what sort of relationship do you have with them? Are you familiar with them?

Are they a source of pleasure . . . or shame . . . or pain . . . or joy? Do you barely notice them at all? Do you honour them as a sacred part of yourself?

Do you know how you like your breasts to be pleasured, either by yourself or by a lover?

Take some more long, slow, deep breaths. Relax your shoulders, your spine and your hips. Again, tune in more deeply to your breasts.

If you were to speak to your breasts, what would you say?

If they responded to you, what would they tell you? What message might they have for you?

Tune in and see if your breasts have an offering for you just now in this moment. Perhaps a word, a sound, a colour, a shape, a message. Something that will remind you of your new connection to this sacred part of your body.

Take some time to listen in for this offering. Trust whatever comes. Take a few more long, slow, deep breaths.

Very slowly, start to bring your awareness to the whole of your body. Stretch gently and wiggle your toes and fingers. Bring your awareness back into the room.

When you are ready, open your eyes. If there was a message from your breasts or if you'd like to remember anything from your journey, take a minute now to write that down in your journal.

90. Genital meditation

"Every desire of your body is holy;
Every desire of your body is Holy." Hafiz

What is your connection to your genitals? How do you feel about them? Most of us grow up in a world that is full of body shame. In particular, we learn to be ashamed of our genitals, how they feel and the desires that arise within them.

Actually, your genitals are a beautiful, gorgeous part of your body. No matter what they look like, they are perfect just as they are. They have the capacity to bring you pleasure, joy and fulfilment.

Some people experience the opposite of that. Fear, shame, and disappointment.

Whether you have a positive relationship with your genitals or not, this meditation will help you to connect in new and deeper ways — to release shame, trauma, and pain, and to invite in pleasure and joy.

You can do this on your own or with a partner.

Find a comfortable place to sit or lie down where you won't be interrupted. Switch off your phone, computer, and other technology. Better yet, don't even have it in the room with you.

Make sure you are warm enough to relax.

Relax your whole body, and in particular, your hips, spine, shoulders and neck. Relax the muscles of your face and jaw. Slow your breathing down. Relax even more.

The only thing you really have to do is be present. Be present with your genitals. Be present and stay present for some time.

The first time you do this, just have the intention to connect to your genitals. To tune into them, be present with them. In future meditations, you can set the intention to get to know them more, to listen deeply to them and even communicate with them.

Continue to relax, and when you are ready, take your awareness to your genitals. You can gently place a hand over them if you wish. Imagine saying hello to them with your mind.

Notice how it feels to do this. What thoughts and feelings arise? Notice if it's easy to stay present in your genitals or if your mind drifts. It's okay if it does, just bring your attention back when you notice that you've drifted.

Use your mind's eye or your inner awareness to trace the outside edges of your genitals. Follow the landscape, the contours and curves. Notice the physicality of them.

If you could hear your genitals speaking with you, what might they say? Can you listen in without any judgement? Without making them wrong or bad? Can you just listen with love?

Remember to breathe deeply and relax all the way through.

When you feel the meditation is finished, send some love down from your heart. Unconditional, Universal love. Send some gratitude too. In this moment, all is well. Breathe that in deeply.

When you do the meditation in the future, you can try one of these:

- Set the intention for your genitals to release and let go of anything which no longer serves them. You don't have to know what is releasing, just trust that it will. You might find yourself yawning, tearing up, or coughing. These are often a sign of release. They won't always happen, but you'll still release whatever needs to go at that time.
- Set the intention to send healing to your genitals. In much the same way as you sent love to your genitals, intend for healing to flow to them now.
- Set the intention to create a deeper relationship with your genitals. Internally, let them know that you are here, present with them. That you want to be closer, own them, create a loving relationship.
- Set the intention to allow pleasure. Whatever and however that looks or feels to you. Imagine allowing your genitals to experience and express pleasure.

- Listen to them! Quite often we assume we know what our genitals would like in terms of healing, attention, and pleasure. But have you ever really listened to them?

We joke about penises having a mind of their own, but there is some truth to that. Not just penises either. All genitals have a kind of consciousness of sorts.

Tune in to yours. Listen deeply with the whole of your being and the whole of your body. Do this repeatedly. Let your genitals learn to trust you to show up. You may 'hear' them by getting a feeling, sensation or intuitive sense. Trust what you experience.

91. Ass/arse/bottom/rear-end/derriere/butt/backside meditation

If you think about the shame we have around our genitals, it's usually even worse for our butts! From the moment we do our very first poop, someone has wrinkled up their nose, made a face, and probably said 'yuck!', referring to the smell. What does that teach us about our bodies and bodily functions?

There's also a lot of shame around enjoying anal sexual pleasure — whatever your gender or sexual preference.

Let me tell you something; your ass is just as sacred as your eyes and arms and heart. Just as precious and pleasurable as your breath.

Find a comfortable place to sit or lie down.

You can sit or lie as normal and still focus on your bottom. If that doesn't feel right, try something else. You could lay on your front, perhaps with a cushion under your hips. You could also be on all fours or with your head and shoulders on a pillow and bottom sticking up.

Relax your whole body, and in particular, your hips, spine, shoulders and neck. Relax the muscles of your face and jaw. Slow your breathing down. Relax even more.

Once again, the only thing you really have to do is be present. Be present with your ass, with your ass cheeks and asshole. Be present and stay present for some time. Notice what thoughts or feelings arise and let them go.

If you want to carry on, then gently place your hands on your butt cheeks or, if you feel drawn to, near or on your asshole. Make sure your hands are clean of course.

Notice how it feels to touch yourself here. How does the rest of your body respond? What thoughts or messages pop up? Remember to breathe and stay present.

If you feel drawn to, send some love down from your heart to your ass. Let it know that you love and accept it as part of you, part of the whole.

As with the genital meditations, you can stop here or add these on:

- Set the intention for your ass to energetically release and let go of anything which no longer serves it. You don't have to know what is releasing, just trust that it will. You might find yourself yawning, tearing up or coughing. These are often a sign of release. There might be some kind of physical release too. That's okay.
- Set the intention to send healing to your ass. In much the same way as you sent love to your ass earlier, intend for healing to flow there now.

- Set the intention to create a deeper relationship with your ass. Internally, let the whole area know that you are here and utterly present. That you want to create a more loving relationship.
- Set the intention to allow pleasure. Whatever and however that looks or feels to you. Imagine allowing your ass to experience pleasure.
- Listen to it! Quite often we assume we know what our body, particularly our ass, would like in terms of healing, attention, and pleasure. But have you ever really listened to it? Tune in now and see what it has to say.

92. Self-pleasuring meditation

What is your relationship to self-pleasuring? To masturbation? Is it something you see as a divine gift, a precious time to honour your body and be devoted to your pleasure? Is it something shameful that you knock out quietly in the shower?

Do you masturbate regularly, rarely, or not at all?

Whatever your current relationship to self-pleasure is, you have the power and capacity to create a new connection. To explore ways of using masturbation as a powerful tool for pleasure, healing, joy, and even magic!

Did you know that whatever you're feeling or thinking about when you are aroused is charged, heightened or reinforced? For example, if you are masturbating and feeling shame, then you are reinforcing shame in your body. If you are masturbating and feeling joy and pleasure, that masturbation is a wonderful thing, then you are reinforcing joy, pleasure and wonder.

Super Simple Self-pleasuring Meditation

The next time you are masturbating, slow down.

Take slower, longer, deeper breaths.

Be utterly present with your body and with the sensations you are feeling. Take your time. Notice the thoughts that arise. If they are negative or shameful, see if you can let them go, or at least not attach to them.

Bring your focus back to your body, to your arousal. See if you can celebrate your pleasure in the present moment.

Super Luxurious Self-pleasuring Meditation

Luxuriating in your own erotic pleasure is a deeply self-loving thing to do. For starters, it helps you keep your own cup full, as it were. Instead of going into intimate situations desperate to get your needs met, you show up already full and overflowing.

It's also a great reminder that pleasure is a birthright, not something you have to earn. It's right there at your fingertips!

Other benefits include:

- A deeper connection with your sensual, sexual self
- More confidence, in and out of the bedroom
- Greater capacity for pleasure
- Improves body awareness and body confidence
- Relieves aches and pains
- Reduces inflammation
- Boosts immune system
- Increases circulation
- Better sleep
- A sense of fulfilment and peace
- Brings you into the present moment!

Set up your space in whatever way feels good to you. Make sure you are warm, comfortable, and won't be disturbed for a while. Turn off all technology. I'd strongly recommend avoiding pornography for this meditation. You are looking to take your energy and awareness inwards, rather than focusing it outwards.

You can make the meditation a bit more special by lighting some candles and setting an intention or two. Your intention could be to connect to your body in a new or a loving way. It could be to remember pleasure, to relax or to connect to a higher power. It can even be to ask the Universe (or whoever you feel comfortable asking) for some guidance, creative energy or healing.

When you're ready, take a few moments to tune into yourself. Relax and take your awareness into your body. How is it feeling? What do you notice? Check in with how you are feeling mentally and emotionally. What's present with you at the moment?

Take some long, slow, deep breaths and relax your body even more. Place one hand on your heart and one hand on your genitals. Allow yourself to just be present with them. You could, if you wanted to, ask the question, 'What do I need in this moment?' and see what your heart, genitals, or body has to say. Trust whatever thoughts or feelings arise.

Follow your intuition as to how your body would like to be touched in this moment. Be super present and listen in more than ever before. Try not to fall back on your default ways of self- pleasuring. Try not to have a goal in mind. You might like to move towards orgasm at some point, but don't assume that's what your body wants. Stay open and curious.

You could:

- Give yourself a full body massage with coconut or other delicious oils.
- Put some music on (or not) and give yourself permission to move your body in sexy, sensual ways. Get your hips moving, arch your back, explore different ways to loosen up your sexual energy and get it flowing.
- Take a warm shower and pay particular attention to the sensuality of the water on your body. Experiment with letting the water stimulate different areas of your body as if it were a lover caressing you. Allow it to 'cradle' your face, to relax your shoulders, to gently stroke your breasts. How does it feel to focus the water on your genitals without having a particular goal in mind?
- Play with making erotic sounds. Moan in pleasure. Make low, deep sounds as you breathe out. Make 'yummy' noises. Play with asking for what you want out loud. Try humming as you raise arousal in your body — see if the vibration of the humming feels good or not. Notice how you feel making erotic noises.
- Keep coming back to your heart as you feel arousal increasing in your body.

- Use your breath to move sexual energy around your body.
- Set an intention for your heightened sexual energy or orgasmic energy. Do *not* direct it at another person. This is for you. Your intention could be to exercise later, to start reading or to finish a project you're working on. Hold the intention in your heart, visualise yourself doing whatever it is that you'd like to do, and then let the intention go. Imagine sending your sexual energy or orgasmic energy towards your intention.
- Be your own best lover. The more you get to know your body and what turns you on, the better lover you'll be. You'll be more confident, more body-aware, and full to overflowing with your own erotic energy.

Take your time, don't be in a rush. Make this an act of self-love.

Take long, slow, deep breaths. Relax your body more than you think you can. Relax your jaw. Allow pleasure to flow. Allow self-love to flow. Allow any emotions arising to flow.

Stay present with your body and with your sexual energy. Delight and revel in the power and pleasure available to you. Get to know it, make friends with it. Whether you choose to share this with someone else or not, it is yours first and foremost. Breathe it in and enjoy it.

Meditations with a Partner

The meditations below provide various ways to connect with your partner. They can be used on their own or combined in whatever way you wish. You can use them as a form of foreplay or at any time.

One of the most important things to bear in mind when doing bedroom meditations with a partner is that it has to be right for both of you at that time. Just because your partner has enjoyed doing one of the meditations previously doesn't mean they're in the mood for them in this moment.

So as always with any form of intimacy, consent is crucial. You want a definite 'hell yes' from your partner rather than an 'I guess so'. If your partner feels obligated in any way, you won't be getting what it is that you're really looking for, and you risk resentment building up.

When you have a 'hell yes', choose which meditation you both want to do and adapt it to suit your mood and needs at the time.

With each of the meditations, you can do as little as five to fifteen minutes or a couple of hours. Choose what feels right at that time for both of you.

Decide whether you're going to take turns giving and receiving or if just one of you is going to give and receive. There is no right or wrong, only what serves you both at that time.

I highly recommend using an alarm to keep firm time boundaries. If you don't stick to the agreed timings, it won't feel good to do another time. Make sure you leave a bit of time for setting up at the beginning and some time to wind down, integrate, cuddle or hug at the end.

93. Eye-gazing

This can be done with a sexual partner, a friend, a child, yourself in the mirror, or even someone you're having a difficulty with.

Over the years of working in the field of conscious sexuality, I would often get asked what my number one tip for better sex would be. My number one tip is to look into each other's eyes and be present.

Sounds simple and obvious, but I've had hundreds of people tell me that they don't do that. That they actively avoid it or that it feels too vulnerable.

Of course, just looking into each other's eyes — if you're not present, if you're stuck in your head or thinking about the shopping — isn't going to work. No one wants to look into vacant eyes.

A few years ago, I took my phone to a shop to get it repaired. They promptly took my phone to the back and asked me to wait. It was a very small shop with three or four staff and a few customers milling about.

While I was waiting, one of the young staff members struck up a conversation with me and asked what I did for a living. I never knew quite how to answer that question, and something different came out every time I was asked.

On this particular occasion, I said, 'I help people have better sex lives'. Usually, one of two things happen when I say something like that. Either the person glazes over and backs away or they perk up and want to share their intimate secrets with me or ask for advice.

On this day, the chap looked at me as if I'd said something important but that it hadn't quite gone in. He muttered a bit of an 'Oh…' and wandered off.

A few minutes later, from across the shop, he looked at me and asked, 'Can you help me?'

I don't know what got into me that day, but I instantly, without thinking about it, said, 'Yeah, come here', and nodded my head to summon him over.

Very tentatively he crossed the shop floor and came to stand in front of me. At this point, some of the customers and most of his work buddies were showing some interest in what was happening.

I told the curious young man to close his eyes and to bring all of himself into this moment. All of the bits he loved and accepted about himself and all of the bits he didn't love and would normally hide.

I told him that I was going to do the same thing, and when he felt ready, I wanted him to open his eyes and that I would be there, ready, and we would just look into each other's eyes.

He shifted his position, rolled his shoulders back and stretched his neck. Then he closed his eyes, and I could feel him bring all of himself into his body and into the moment. I did the same.

After a moment or two, he opened his eyes and we met, eye to eye, on the shop floor. Both of us fully present, both of us bringing all of who we were, not hiding anything.

It was intense and beautiful and ecstatic in those few seconds. It was deeply intimate. It wasn't sexual, but could have been if that had been our intent.

After only a few seconds, he broke the eye contact exclaiming, 'Wow! Wow! What did you do? That was amazing! I'm going to tell my girlfriend!' And with that, he wandered off to phone her.

When (if) we look into someone's eyes, whether we know them or not, we often (usually) only show them the parts of ourselves that we like or feel comfortable to show or that we feel is good enough.

That's fine if you're not looking to make a connection or don't feel safe.

However, if you really want to experience deep intimacy, if you want to connect with someone, whether for erotic reasons or not, you have to be willing to bring all of you into the moment.

The good, the bad, and the ugly.

One of my teachers used to say, "Intimacy is into-me-see'. Letting someone see you fully.

When two people only bring what they deem 'good enough' to the moment, half of who they are is left behind. So you end up with a half-ass, surface connection where neither party feels safe enough to bring all of who they are.

Imagine showing all of who you are to your partner and being loved and accepted in that moment. What a deep moment of true intimacy.

There is also a magical energy exchange that happens when you gaze, fully present, into someone's eyes.

When we see someone out in the world, or even someone we've lived with for twenty-five years, we tend to notice the outer features of that person. We see the shape of their face, their hair, all the predominant physical features.

How often do you stop to look beyond that? To look beyond the physical to see who is really there? Who is living in that body, who is behind that face and those eyes?

As you gaze into your partner's eyes, look beyond the physical.

Be present with whatever arises, without preference or judgement.

Sometimes, when you're gazing into your partner's eyes, it might appear as if their face changes, or it might seem a bit blurry. Be open and curious and just bear witness. Stay present.

You can either set a timer for this or just allow it to end naturally. If you do set a timer, start with two or three minutes. You can increase the time as you feel more comfortable.

Note: Eye-gazing with your eyes closed

Many years ago, I attended a tantra workshop with a friend. My partner couldn't make it and I really wanted to do this particular class. A friend of mine agreed to come with me, thankfully.

One of the exercises was eye-gazing. She and I had both done this on a previous tantra course we attended, but we'd never done it with each other. As we sat facing each other, cross-legged on the floor, she told me that she wasn't always comfortable to have her eyes open, but that she would absolutely be 100 percent present with me.

The teacher guided us through getting settled and in our bodies. We were invited to close our eyes to get centred and present. Eventually, we were invited to open our eyes and to gaze into our partner's eyes.

I opened my eyes as instructed and gazed upon my friend's face. At first, I felt a bit of disappointment that she wasn't going to open her eyes. As I just allowed that feeling to be there, I became aware of something. It was her absolute full presence. It was almost as if she were looking at me through her eyelids somehow. I gazed at her closed eyes just as I would have if her eyes were open. I was utterly present with her.

From time to time she'd open her eyes, her presence never shifting, and then gently close them again. It was extremely powerful.

If you or your partner isn't comfortable with full eye-gazing, then allow your eyes to open and close at will. The most important thing is to stay absolutely present in the moment.

I've also done eye-gazing with blind and partially sighted people. The same thing applies; however, in my experience, you might offer to have a bit of physical contact. It could just be your knees touching or a very light hand-holding or hands on each other's knees. It's not essential though. Experiment with different things to find out what works and doesn't work for you in that moment.

94. Dusting Off the Day

This is a beautiful meditation to do at the end of the day — or anytime you feel like it!

It is a great way to get present with each other, to let go of the stress and detritus of the day, and to prepare to be more 'naked' and ready to connect with each other.

It's also a sensual and intimate way to connect with each other without full sex. It's relaxing, healing and allows you both to feel loved and cared for.

Create a comfortable space where one of you can lie down and the other can be sitting. Before you begin, sit opposite each other and take a few minutes to drop into the space. Do some breathing and eye-gazing together.

Decide who is going first and invite them to lie face down.

If you are the giver, take your awareness into your heart and connect with Universal, unconditional love. Allow that energy to travel down your arms and into your hands so that your hands are messengers of your heart.

You are now in service to your partner. Gently place your hand over your partner's heart. Take a moment to connect to their heart.

While that's happening, the receiver sets the intention to let go of anything which no longer serves them.

Then, starting with the back of the head, the giver uses a very light touch to brush or dust the energy off the receiver's body. Tune in and trust your intuition.

Work your way down the neck, shoulders and arms. Pay particular attention to places that feel 'sticky' or where the receiver says feels like it needs a bit more focus.

Move down the spine, being aware of the organs inside the body. Move down the lower back, hips and bottom. Eventually work your way down the backs of the legs, ankles and feet.

Repeat two or three times or until you both feel the back of the body is complete. Before you ask the receiver to turn over, do two or three long, sweeping brush strokes all the way from the top of the head to the bottom of the feet.

Ask the receiver to turn over and do the same down the front of the body.

When you do the face, use an even lighter touch, lighter than you think you need to. Ask your partner if the pressure you're using feels right. Adjust to whatever is comfortable for them.

If this sort of healing/clearing work is familiar to you, you might like to set your intention for the Universe, source or whatever feels comfortable to you to clear whatever is ready to go or for your highest good — then lie back and trust the process in silence.

If you're not sure about that or if it helps you to specifically name the things you want to let go of, then start stating these things out loud while your partner brushes you off. You might say, 'I'm letting go of stress', 'I'm letting go of fear', 'I am letting go of pain ...' or whatever else you are aware of wanting to let go of.

For some people, verbalising these intentions helps it to feel more concrete, more tangible. Whichever way you choose, it will still be working. Do what feels right for you.

Once you've both received, take a moment or two to share how it felt to receive and how you're feeling now.

Note: If you are doing this with someone who prefers not to be touched (or if you don't want to touch them), you can do the whole process with your hands above their body. Check in with each other before you begin so you know each other's boundaries and what feels right at this time.

95. Placing affirmations in the body

This can stand alone or be a continuation of the 'Dusting Off the Day' meditation.

If starting fresh, start by sitting opposite each other, doing some eye-gazing and taking a few minutes to get present and in your body. Allow your hearts to open and connect.

Have a quiet conversation about who is going to receive first, and then what affirmations or positive words or phrases they'd like to receive. When you're ready, the receiver lies face down. Take a moment to get totally comfortable and relaxed.

The giver sits next to them and prepares by taking a few deep breaths and relaxing their body. Take your awareness into your heart and connect with the Universal, unconditional love energy there.

Allow or imagine that energy travelling out from your heart to your arms, then down to your hands. Your hands become messengers of your heart. You are now in service to your partner.

Gently place your hand over your partner's heart and take a moment to connect to the love there.

When you feel connected and ready, ask them for their first statement or affirmation.

Some possibilities include:

- I am loved.
- I am worthy.
- I am magnificent.
- I am strong.
- I am capable.
- I am open to receiving.
- I am successful.

Hold your hands out and invite the energy or quality of their affirmation to come into your hands. You may or may not feel some warmth or tingling in your hands.

Slowly, gently, and lovingly, place your full palm, full of this quality, onto their body. Hold your palm still as their body absorbs the affirmation or statement.

Continue to move your affirmation-infused hands all around their body.

They can tell you to change to a new affirmation whenever they wish.

The receiver decides if and when they wish to turn on to their back. It's really great to cover both sides of the body, but it's not essential.

Keep going until the receiver feels complete. Allow the receiver some time to just be still and integrate it all.

You can swap over now or another time. When you are completely finished, share your experiences of giving and receiving.

96. The naked embrace

There are a million reasons why a naked embrace with your beloved partner is good for you. Science shows that an embrace or hug that lasts just twenty seconds releases oxytocin, the bonding hormone. Oxytocin is released in women who've just had babies. It creates feelings of love and trust. It is also an anti-inflammatory, so can help with aches and pains in the body.

A naked embrace can help regulate your heart rate and breathing, calm your nervous system, and reduce stress and anxiety. Making the time for a naked embrace can increase self-worth, confidence, and most of all, increase intimacy!

You can start with both of you already undressed or include time to undress each other. Once you are both naked, take a moment to stand or lie down across from each other without touching.

Look into each other's eyes. Bring your full self to the moment and into your eyes. Allow your partner to witness all of you through your eyes while you do the same for them. Just two or three long breaths is plenty, and you can do longer if you wish.

Slowly move towards each other and bring your bodies together fully. Have your left hand rest gently on their lower back and your right hand rest behind their heart centre.

Relax and breathe. Open your heart and allow love to flow.

You may or may not experience arousal. Either way is fine. For the time that you agreed to be in an embrace, just allow the arousal to be there without having to do anything in particular with it.

When the agreed time is over, you can go on about your day or move into lovemaking if you both wish to.

97. The simple chakra touch meditation

This meditation can be done fully clothed, partially clothed, or completely naked. Decide what feels right for you both. Choose if you're each going to give and receive or only one of you. Set your timer accordingly.

Once you are ready, the first giver invites the first receiver to lie down, face up. The rest of these instructions are for the giver.

Invite your partner to take two long, slow, deep breaths and to relax their body on the out-breath.

Do this round without any touch.

Bring your full presence to witnessing their breathing and breathe with them, at their own pace.

Once they've done two full breaths, place your dominant hand (the hand you write with) lightly over their genitals (this is the base chakra) and both of you bring your attention/awareness/mind's eye to the area.

Rest there for a moment and then both of you take two long, slow, deep breaths. The giver aligns their breath with the receiver's breath. Rest for another moment, then move to the belly.

Repeat the whole process at each of the other chakras (energy centres in the body).

They are:

Belly - The soft part of the belly under the belly button.
Solar plexus - Just below the sternum, over the stomach.
Heart - In the centre of the chest. Remember, this is the heart chakra, not the actual heart.
Throat - You guessed it! At throat level — be very gentle with your touch here. You can even hold your hand above it rather than touching it if necessary.
Third eye - Also known as the brow chakra. This is located just in-between and a little above your eyebrows.
Crown - The top of your head and a bit above it.
When you've been through all of them, ask your partner if they'd like to return to any of the places. If so, go back and do two more breaths there.

When it feels complete, remove your hand and both of you take two more breaths. Give them time to let it all sink in. If you are swapping over, do so slowly, gently, and with as little talking as possible.

Once you've both received and the whole process feels complete, cuddle up and rest together.

98. Moving breath between you

There are a few ways to do this one. You want to be facing each other in whatever way is most comfortable for you both. You can be standing up, lying down or sitting in chairs.

You can also have one partner sit on the floor or bed, cross-legged, with a pillow or cushion on their ankles. The other partner would then sit on the cushion, facing them, with their legs wrapped around the waist of their partner. You would both have your arms around each other.

Start by looking into each other's eyes. Be as fully present as you can in each moment.

If you're able to, allow your hips to start to rock, very, very gently, in a slight thrusting movement or side to side.

Move your focus and awareness on to your own hip and genital area. Rock your hips and take long, slow deep breaths. You may or may not feel a warmth, tingling, buzzing, something else or nothing at all. Don't worry, just keep going.

Imagine that you are breathing in from your partner's genital area into your own and breathing out from yours to theirs. Take at least three breaths here.

Nod your head to let your partner know when you each feel ready to move on. When you are both ready, move your focus and awareness up to the belly. Allow the movement to start to come from the belly area. Breathe in from your partner's belly into yours and out from yours to theirs.

As before, take at least three long breaths together. When you are both ready, keep moving your focus and attention upwards. At each level, take at least three breaths together. Breathe in from their body to yours and out from yours to theirs.

Keep doing this up through the solar plexus, heart, throat, third eye and crown. Stay connected with your eyes throughout. Do this in silence if you can.

When you've completed the breathing at the crown, become aware of how your body is feeling. Check in with each other with as few words as possible.

You can stop there, repeat the whole process, move on to cuddling or lovemaking, or do whatever you feel drawn to do afterwards.

Don't rush. Stay close to each other for a bit afterwards, maybe cuddle up or spoon. Be sure to have some water afterwards.

99. Partnered genital gazing meditation

So often, one of the only experiences we have of our genitals, in terms of partnered pleasure, is of that person wanting something from our genitals.

Often the erotic experience is shrunk down to getting the genitals ready for penetration. You do this to me and I do that to you so that our genitals are ready for what we narrowly call sex.

This meditation offers you the experience of your genitals being loved and appreciated without anything being required of them.

It is much more powerful than it sounds.

Generally, it's okay to see each other's shoulders or ankles or belly buttons, but not genitals. Why? Shame.

Most people carry shame in their genitals. Think about it — as soon as we are born, a nappy is slapped on us and from there on out we are expected to keep ourselves covered.

There is a deep shame and conditioning about how our genitals should look and smell and act. If yours aren't doing exactly the right thing (and believe me, most people think theirs are wrong/bad/deformed/ugly), then you are somehow not worthy, not good enough.

It breaks my heart. Truly.

Let me tell you something.

Whatever your genitals look like, however they smell or taste or look or feel or act — they are beautiful, and they are perfect. Just like you.

How to Do This Meditation

Create a safe, sacred space where you won't be disturbed. Agree on a time boundary. Ideally, you'd have at least fifteen minutes to give and to receive.

The person who's going to share their genitals first lies down and gets comfortable. If desired, they can have a towel, blanket, or sarong covering their genitals to start with. They can be otherwise dressed or naked, however you both feel most comfortable and safe.

The person who's going to be the observer first sits nearby. Be as comfortable as possible so that there's little fidgeting during the meditation. The observer can be clothed, partially clothed, or naked, so long as both partners agree as to what feels right.

Once you're both settled and comfortable, the observer sets a timer for the agreed time and sets it aside.

The person being observed may wear a blindfold if they wish. This isn't so they can check out and not be present. Not at all. This is only if it helps them to relax and feel more present in their body and especially, in their genitals.

Both of you start to take long, slow, deep breaths and relax your bodies. When the sharer is ready, they remove anything covering their genitals. More deep breaths and relaxing for both partners.

The observer 'looks through the eyes of their heart' at their partner's genitals. What does that mean to look through the eyes of your heart? It means to look through the eyes of love and compassion rather than judgment, shame or fear. Open your heart, drop your awareness into it, and imagine that you can look through the eyes of love.

Be very aware of how vulnerable it can be to have your genitals on show like this. Allowing someone you trust to gaze lovingly at your genitals, without engaging or trying to get something from them, can be very moving, very profound.

It can also feel funny, strange, erotic, stimulating, scary, or a million other things. Whatever you experience is okay. There is no right or wrong way.

If 'stuff' comes up, for either person, you can choose whether to continue with the meditation or ask for a pause. Don't suffer silently. Also, don't just disappear without telling your partner what is going on.

When the timer goes off, allow the person being observed to come back into contact in their own time. When they are ready, take a moment or two to eye-gaze, with gratitude in your eyes. Stay in silence.

Very gently swap over. Keep talking to an absolute minimum, and only about anything needed in the swap over. You will debrief afterwards. Don't forget to reset the timer.

When both of you have had a turn in each direction, sit or lie quietly together. Cuddle if you wish. When you are ready, share how it was both to give and to receive. Remember to speak from your heart, with kindness and compassion.

Note: You can (and should!) do this on your own too. It is very powerful to observe your own genitals, without judgement, preference or shame. You can keep it very simple and informal by just gazing at your genitals during your shower or when you use the loo. Do it with love and your full presence. Have your heart open and a curious mind.

Better yet, make time for this meditation to be something special. Grab a handheld mirror and take your time gazing, with love, at your genitals. Notice what comes up for you and gently let it pass through. If you wish to, use a tender touch to help you see more of your genitals. Allow yourself to gently explore your own shapes, contours and textures. It doesn't have to be a sexual experience unless you want it to. Send love and gratitude to your genitals before you finish.

100. Witnessing your partner's self-pleasuring

This is a beautiful meditation to do. It allows you to hold sacred space for your partner's pleasure while observing and learning how they pleasure themselves.

Usually, you are a part of the action, so you don't get to witness your partner separately from what you are doing close to the action, as it were.

Set up just as you would for the meditation above. The first 'self-pleasurer' might also wish to have lube, toys or something else available. Gather whatever you need and have them near you before you begin.

Just as in the 'Genital Gazing' meditation, the observer does not touch or get involved. They also don't pleasure themselves during this part. Their turn comes later.

The 'self-pleasurer' can make sounds as they wish (I highly encourage it!); however, the observer stays silent. Deep breathing is good for both of you.

The self-pleasurer decides whether or not they wish to orgasm and when they feel their turn is complete.

Change over with as little chatter as possible.

Remember to hold sacred space for each other, to observe from your heart, and to be kind and compassionate.

When you've both had a turn, cuddle up and gently share how it was for you — both as the witness and the 'pleasurer'.

101. Leaning into the bubble of love

This meditation is deep and delightful in all sorts of ways. It gives each of you a chance to relax into the other, to give and receive, to deepen trust, and to feel held and nurtured.

Create a comfortable space where one of you can sit down, legs spread open, back supported by a wall or piece of furniture that won't move. Use as many cushions or pillows as you need to be comfortable.

To begin, sit or stand opposite each other. Do some eye-gazing and slow breathing together. Get centred, grounded, and totally present.

When you're both ready, have the first 'giver' sit comfortably, with their back supported. Once they're in place, they silently invite their partner to sit, with their back leaning into the chest of the giver. So you are both facing the same way — the 'giver' with their back up against the wall and the 'receiver' leaning into their partner. Take a moment to each get comfortable.

When you've both settled, the 'giver' places their arms gently around the 'receiver'. Left hand on their belly and right hand over their heart. If you can't reach, that's totally fine. Just hold your partner lovingly.

Continue to relax into this holding. Slow your breathing.

Each of you take your awareness into your heart. Feel the unconditional, Universal love flowing there. Allow your heart to expand. Feel this love flowing out behind you, in front of you, to the sides of you, and eventually meeting the love flowing from your partner. Imagine this becomes a big bubble of love, one that envelops, enriches and holds you both.

Eventually, the 'giver' starts to deepen their breathing, and the 'receiver' follows their rhythm and pace.

As the 'giver', slow your breathing down. The deeper and slower you go, the more relaxed you will both become. Do this for as long as feels right. When it feels complete, each of you take three deep breaths at your own pace.

Slowly and gently come to sitting opposite each other. Look into your partner's eyes with love.

You can change over or not, depending on what feels right to you at the time.

Final Thoughts

So there you have it — 101 meditations for life, business and bedroom success.

One hundred and one ways to connect more intimately with your heart and soul, with the things that give you joy, with nature, your senses, with your full self and with others. One hundred and one ways to come into the present moment, no matter where you are or what you're doing.

Being present, or in the 'now', is all there really is. We can be present with anything and everything we do, feel, say and be. When you are fully in the moment, your senses are heightened, intimacy is deepened, and you feel vibrant and alive.

Whether you started this book thinking you had to sit still and empty your mind to meditate or you've been practising meditation in various ways for years, I hope you've found something of value here. Something that resonates for you and will help you practice being in the moment more regularly.

You can meditate on your own, with a child or friend, with a sexual partner, and with groups of people too. You can open a business meeting by asking everyone to take a long slow deep breath. You can connect more deeply with a lover by taking a moment to consciously look into each other's eyes. You can deepen self-awareness and increase confidence by focusing inwards, listening to your body and intuition, and trusting what you hear and feel.

Meditating can be as quick and simple as just noticing that you're breathing or as advanced as coordinating your breath with a partner, luxuriating in a barefoot walk or a self-pleasuring ritual. It can be formal or informal. There really is no 'right' or 'wrong' way. Explore, experiment, and see what works best for you in the moment.

Gratitude

This book would not be in your hands right now without the love, help and support from these gorgeous souls. I am deeply grateful to everyone that has helped, encouraged, held my hand and gently nudged me to get this out into the world.

Guy Johnson - for sparking the original idea for this book in the first place!

Todd - for believing in me, encouraging me, listening to me, and loving me while I paced and pondered and birthed this book.

Hannah - for always loving and supporting me.

My momma – for bringing me to life and inspiring the toaster meditation!

Seani Love – for tweaking the title and making it better.

Michele Freedman, Stephen McParlin, Jackie Chappell, Steve Jones, Martin Warwillow, and Tim Johnson - for giving so freely of their time, focus and energy in proofreading/copy editing the book. Special love and shout out to Tim Johnson who offered invaluable advice, comments and help long after he needed to.

Glynis and Andy Roache - for figuring out self-publishing so that I could follow in their footsteps and attach my book wagon to your publishing house star.

Avanti Shivpuri - for seeing that writing this book nourished my soul, even when it was difficult. Without that reminder I might have given up.

Mollena Williams Haas - for the kick up the butt to finally publish the book!

To all of my teachers, past and present.

To the creative muses, stars, Mumma tree and the ancient golden Priestess for always supporting me and whispering in my ear when I needed it.

About the Author

What friends had to say:

Heather Keefe Cella: Rebecca Gwyn – soul of a poet and dreamer since childhood. Allegiant to honesty and to the beauty of imperfections. Rebecca, my precious childhood companion, is someone who whispers her truth humbly and graciously accepts the world as it whispers back.

Rachel Goldberg: "Rebecca is the best seeeester on the planet…" (My sis, obvs)

Dawn Thompson Garren: "You are just so real. I could write a book about your generous spirit and heart."

Stephanie Jane Hemsted: "Real. Practical. Down to earth. Open-hearted."

Karianne Kat Fagan: "My go to gal for all things magical and beautiful and engaging."

Short version:

Rebecca was born and raised in the US and has lived in the UK since 1987. She has been a personal and professional explorer of intimacy, sexuality, pleasure, energy, healing, bodywork, consciousness, magic, and more for over twenty-five years.

For the last thirteen years, she has been known as 'The Sexual Alchemist'. As such, she has offered powerful sessions and programs helping men transform, expand and explore their ideas and experiences of who they are as sexual beings.

Rebecca has a wonderful daughter and lives in London with her delicious partner. She loves walking in nature, raw chocolate, hot, sunny beaches and piles of blankets — though not at the same time!

Longer version:

Rebecca was born in Dallas, Texas, raised in Memphis, Tennessee, and moved to London, UK in 1987.

With an Honours degree in Human Services, Rebecca delved into the world of care work for a few years, working mostly with autistic children and adults with learning difficulties.

In 1992, she came across a book on Nichiren Shoshu Buddhism. The book talked about chanting as a way of connecting to the divine, as a way of aligning oneself with oneness. The idea of chanting didn't really resonate for her, but she quickly recognised the feeling or experience that they were describing as what was happening for her on the dance floor and, if she was really lucky, during sex.

This experience was a major catalyst in Rebecca's journey. For the next twenty years, Rebecca explored and studied how the body and mind work together, how energy works in and through the body, massage, reflexology, reiki, energy healing, intuitive healing, and more.

About fifteen years ago, she came across a tantra workshop at a festival. It was only a two-hour introduction, but afterwards something inside her had changed forever.

Rebecca went on to study tantra with the teacher from the festival. Early on in the course, the teacher remarked, 'You already know this stuff. You just don't know what you know'. It was true, something in Rebecca was awakening.

Soon after the course, people started asking her for 'sexual alchemy' sessions, and a new business was born.

Rebecca now offers Sexual Alchemy and Keys to the Kingdom programs for men who want to explore and expand their potential for pleasure, connection and intimacy.

Using an intuitive combination of bodywork, conscious touch, various healing methods, counselling, breathwork, conscious awareness, meditation, sex magic and ritual, neo-tantra and conscious kink, Rebecca is the catalyst for powerful, magical transformations.

Her most powerful offering, The Keys to the Kingdom, is a four-, or twelve-month program that fully supports your total transformation into a conscious, powerful, masterful lover and King.

Rebecca has a fabulous, grown-up daughter and lives in London with her totally delicious partner of eleven years.

She loves walking in nature, magic, rituals, raw chocolate, tattoos, Prince (and is still not quite over his early death), walking on a hot, sunny beach, or snuggling up in front of a fire under warm blankets.

Hang out with Rebecca online in these places:

Rebeccalowrie.com

Facebook
https://www.facebook.com/rebecca.lowrie1

LinkedIn
https://www.linkedin.com/in/rebeccalowrie/

Twitter
https://twitter.com/

Instagram
https://www.instagram.com/selfalchemy/

"Whatever you do mindfully is meditation".
Thich Nhat Hanh

Printed in Great Britain
by Amazon